Better Homes and Gardens

8 GRAMS or LESS LOW-CARB RECIPES

Meredith® Books
Des Moines, Iowa

8 Grams or Less Low-Carb Recipes

Editor: Jan Miller, R.D.
Contributing Editor: Mary Williams
Senior Associate Design Director: Mick Schnepf
Contributing Designer: Brad Ruppert, Studio G
Copy Chief: Terri Fredrickson
Publishing Operations Manager: Karen Schirm
Edit and Design Production Coordinator: Mary Lee Gavin
Book Production Managers: Pam Kvitne, Marjorie J. Schenkelberg, Rick von Holdt, Mark Weaver
Contributing Copy Editor: Kim Catanzarite
Contributing Proofreaders: Emmy C. Clausing, Susan J. Kling, Gretchen Kauffman
Indexer: Elizabeth Parson
Editorial Assistant: Cheryl Eckert
Test Kitchen Director: Lynn Blanchard
Test Kitchen Product Supervisor: Juliana Hale
Test Kitchen Home Economists: Paige Boyle; Marilyn Cornelius; Laura Harms, R.D.;
    Jennifer Kalinowski, R.D.; Maryellyn Krantz; Jill Moberly; Dianna Nolin; Colleen Weeden;
    Lori Wilson; Charles Worthington
Recipe Developers: Linda J. Henry, Tami Leonard, Marcia Stanley

Meredith® Books
Editor in Chief: Linda Raglan Cunningham
Design Director: Matt Strelecki
Managing Editor: Gregory H. Kayko
Executive Editor: Jennifer Dorland Darling

Publisher: James D. Blume
Executive Director, Marketing: Jeffrey Myers
Executive Director, New Business Development: Todd M. Davis
Executive Director, Sales: Ken Zagor
Director, Operations: George A. Susral
Director, Production: Douglas M. Johnston
Business Director: Jim Leonard

Vice President and General Manager: Douglas J. Guendel

***Better Homes and Gardens®* Magazine**
Editor in Chief: Karol DeWulf Nickell
Deputy Editor, Food and Entertaining: Nancy Hopkins

Meredith Publishing Group
President, Publishing Group: Stephen M. Lacy
Vice President-Publishing Director: Bob Mate

Meredith Corporation
Chairman and Chief Executive Officer: William T. Kerr

In Memoriam: E.T. Meredith III (1933-2003)

Our seal assures you that every recipe in *8 Grams or Less Low-Carb Recipes* has been tested in the Better Homes and Gardens® Test Kitchen. This means that each recipe is practical and reliable, and meets our high standards of taste appeal. We guarantee your satisfaction with this book for as long as you own it.

All of us at Meredith® Books are dedicated to providing you with the information and ideas you need to create delicious foods. We welcome your comments and suggestions. Write to us at: Meredith Books, Cookbook Editorial Department, 1716 Locust St., Des Moines, IA 50309-3023.

If you would like to purchase any of our cooking, crafts, gardening, home improvement, or home decorating and design books, check wherever quality books are sold. Or visit us at: bhgbooks.com

Pictured on front cover: Barbecued Baby Back Ribs (see recipe, page 42)

Low-carb living is easy!

Getting a low-carb dinner on the table has never been easier. *Better Homes and Gardens® 8 Grams or Less Low Carb Recipes* offers more than 200 simply delicious recipes to add variety and inspiration to everyday meals.

A quick flip through the pages of this book allows you to plan your carbohydrate intake for the entire day. You'll find the net carbs (total grams of carbohydrates minus grams of dietary fiber) at the top of each page. Choose from satisfying breakfasts, savory snacks, delicious main dishes, and delectable side dishes—the menu possibilities are endless.

If you've reached the maintenance phase of your diet and can enjoy a more liberal carbohydrate level, check out the selection of recipes in the back of the book that contain up to 15 grams net carbs, and it includes a few mouthwatering desserts!

The best news? Most recipes call for five simple-to-find ingredients—no trips to special markets required. In some cases a recipe calls for such low-carbohydrate products as barbecue sauce or catsup. A quick trip to this rapidly growing section of your supermarket will provide what you need. In most cases the recipes in this book feature common convenience products such as pasta sauce, canned tomato products, and salad dressings. Compare the food manufacturers' nutrition and ingredient labels and purchase those products with the least amount of added sugar (if any).

Finally, each recipe includes a complete nutritional analysis. The Nutrition Facts and Daily Values were calculated with computer software, and values were rounded to the nearest whole number. The analyses don't include optional ingredients. When ingredient choices appear (such as olive oil and butter), the first one mentioned is used for analysis. Also, the first serving size listed is analyzed when a range is given. Pay close attention to serving sizes because carbs quickly add up if portions are too generous.

Meal planning for a low-carb lifestyle doesn't have to be boring and routine. Take a peek inside and get cooking! Enjoy the exciting variety of flavors these dishes will bring to your table.

chapter 1

Beef, Pork, and Lamb

Basil-Garlic Sirloin Roast

Start the roast in a hot oven (425°F) to give the outside of the meat a rich brown color and to seal in the flavorful juices. Finish the roast at a lower temperature to keep the meat fork-tender.

Prep: 15 minutes Roast: 50 minutes Stand: 10 minutes Oven: 425°F/350°F
Makes: 10 to 12 servings

- 1   3- to 3½-pound boneless beef sirloin roast, cut 1¾ inches thick
- ¼   teaspoon salt
- ¼   teaspoon black pepper
- 2   cups lightly packed fresh basil leaves, snipped
- 8   to 10 cloves garlic, minced (2 tablespoons)
- 2   teaspoons olive oil

1 Make five or six 5-inch-long slits along the top of the roast, cutting almost through it. Sprinkle roast with salt and pepper. In a small bowl combine basil and garlic; stuff into slits in roast. Tie roast with clean heavy-duty string to hold slits closed. Drizzle with olive oil.

2 Place meat on a rack in a shallow roasting pan. Insert a meat thermometer into center of meat. Roast in a 425° oven for 15 minutes. Reduce oven temperature to 350°. Roast for 35 to 45 minutes more or until desired doneness (160°F for medium). Cover and let stand for 10 minutes before carving.

Nutrition Facts per serving: 255 cal., 13 g total fat (5 g sat. fat), 91 mg chol., 121 mg sodium, 1 g carbo., 0 g fiber, 31 g pro.
Daily Values: 23% iron

Quick Onion and Herb Pot Roast

Sautéed onion and garlic lend their home-cooked flavor to a premade, store-bought pot roast.

Prep: 5 minutes Cook: 15 minutes Makes: 4 servings
- 1 large onion, thinly sliced
- 1 clove garlic, minced
- 1 tablespoon butter
- 1 16- or 17-ounce package refrigerated cooked beef pot roast with juices
- 2 teaspoons snipped fresh basil, oregano, and/or thyme
  Salt and black pepper

1 In a large skillet cook onion and garlic in hot butter over medium heat about 5 minutes until nearly tender. Add pot roast with juices. Bring to boiling; reduce heat. Simmer, covered, about 10 minutes or until pot roast is heated through.

2 Transfer pot roast to a serving platter, reserving juices in skillet. Stir basil into skillet; season to taste with salt and pepper. Pour juices over pot roast.

Nutrition Facts per serving: 213 cal., 11 g total fat (5 g sat. fat), 72 mg chol., 488 mg sodium, 6 g carbo., 1 g fiber, 24 g pro.
Daily Values: 3% vit. A, 5% vit. C, 1% calcium, 9% iron

net carbs **1**

Lime-Cilantro Flank Steak

If you like fajitas and can afford the carbs, cut the grilled flank steak into thin slices and wrap in low-carb tortillas.

Prep: 15 minutes Marinate: 2 hours Grill: 17 minutes Makes: 6 servings
- 1 1½-pound beef flank steak
- 2 limes
- 1 cup loosely packed fresh cilantro leaves
- ½ teaspoon salt
- ¼ to ½ teaspoon cayenne pepper
- 3 cloves garlic, minced

1 Trim fat from steak. Score steak on both sides by making shallow cuts at 1-inch intervals in a diamond pattern. Place steak in a self-sealing plastic bag set in a shallow dish. Finely shred lime peel until you have 1 tablespoon peel. Cut limes in half; squeeze the lime halves until you have 3 tablespoons juice.

2 For marinade, in a blender container or food processor bowl combine lime peel, lime juice, cilantro, salt, cayenne pepper, and garlic. Cover and blend or process until almost smooth. Pour over steak; seal bag. Marinate in the refrigerator for 2 hours, turning bag occasionally.

3 Drain steak, discarding marinade. For a charcoal grill, grill steak on the rack of an uncovered grill directly over medium coals for 17 to 21 minutes for medium (160°F), turning once halfway through grilling. (For a gas grill, preheat grill. Reduce heat to medium. Place steak on grill rack over heat. Cover and grill as above.) To serve, thinly slice steak diagonally across the grain into thin strips.

Nutrition Facts per serving: 177 cal., 8 g total fat (3 g sat. fat), 56 mg chol., 271 mg sodium, 2 g carbo., 1 g fiber, 23 g pro.
Daily Values: 16% vit. A, 14% vit. C, 2% calcium, 4% iron

Peppered Tenderloins with Asiago Cheese

Prep: 5 minutes Cook: 10 minutes Makes: 4 servings

- 4 beef tenderloin steaks, cut 1 inch thick
- 1 teaspoon coarsely ground black pepper
- 1 tablespoon butter
- 1 ounce Asiago cheese, shaved
- ¼ cup beef broth

1 Rub both sides of steaks with pepper. In a large skillet melt butter over medium-high heat. Add steaks. Reduce heat to medium and cook for 10 to 13 minutes, turning steaks halfway through cooking (145°F for medium rare or 160°F for medium). Transfer steaks to a serving platter, reserving drippings in skillet. Top steaks with cheese; keep warm.

2 Add beef broth to skillet. Cook and stir until bubbly to loosen any browned bits in bottom of skillet. Pour over steaks.

Nutrition Facts per serving: 294 cal., 18 g total fat (8 g sat. fat), 103 mg chol., 225 mg sodium, 1 g carbo., 0 g fiber, 31 g pro.
Daily Values: 2% vit. A, 7% calcium, 22% iron

Lemon Pepper Steaks

Round out this flavorful steak with a side of grilled veggies. Quartered sweet peppers, sliced eggplant, or quartered zucchini or yellow summer squash make savory accompaniments. Brush the vegetables with olive oil before grilling.

Prep: 10 minutes Grill: 11 minutes Makes: 4 servings

- 2 boneless beef top loin steaks, cut 1 inch thick
- 1 tablespoon snipped fresh oregano or 1 teaspoon dried oregano, crushed
- 1 teaspoon bottled minced garlic
- 1 teaspoon finely shredded lemon peel
- 1 teaspoon olive oil or cooking oil
- ¼ teaspoon coarsely ground black pepper

1 Trim fat from steaks. In a small bowl stir together oregano, garlic, lemon peel, oil, and pepper. Using your fingers, rub mixture onto both sides of steaks.

2 For a charcoal grill, grill steaks on rack of an uncovered grill directly over medium coals until desired doneness, turning meat once halfway through grilling. Allow 11 to 15 minutes for medium rare (145°F) and 14 to 18 minutes for medium (160°F). (For a gas grill, preheat grill. Reduce heat to medium. Place steak on grill rack over heat. Cover and grill as above.) To serve, thinly slice steak diagonally across the grain into thin strips.

Broiling Directions: Preheat broiler. Place steaks on the unheated rack of a broiler pan. Broil 3 to 4 inches from heat until desired doneness, turning once halfway through broiling. Allow 12 to 14 minutes for medium rare and 15 to 18 minutes for medium.

Nutrition Facts per serving: 154 cal., 5 g total fat (2 g sat. fat), 54 mg chol., 61 mg sodium, 1 g carbo., 0 g fiber, 24 g pro.
Daily Values: 3% vit. C, 2% calcium, 48% iron

Beef Steaks with Blue Cheese and Walnuts

A cool topping of pungent blue cheese, tangy sour cream, and crunchy walnuts makes a tasty condiment for these pan-broiled steaks.

Prep: 10 minutes Cook: 10 minutes Makes: 4 servings
- 4   beef tenderloin steaks, cut 1 inch thick
- ½   teaspoon garlic salt
-     Nonstick cooking spray
- ⅓   cup dairy sour cream
- 3   tablespoons crumbled blue cheese
- 3   tablespoons chopped toasted walnuts

1 Sprinkle both sides of steaks with garlic salt. Lightly coat a large skillet with cooking spray. Heat skillet over medium-high heat. Add steaks. Reduce heat to medium and cook for 10 to 13 minutes or until desired doneness, turning steaks halfway through cooking (145°F for medium rare or 160°F for medium). Transfer steaks to a serving platter.

2 Meanwhile, in a small bowl stir together sour cream and blue cheese; spoon on top of steaks. Sprinkle with walnuts.

Nutrition Facts per serving: 264 cal., 17 g total fat (6 g sat. fat), 81 mg chol., 255 mg sodium, 2 g carbo., 0 g fiber, 26 g pro.
Daily Values: 3% vit. A, 6% calcium, 18% iron

4 net carbs

Grilled BLT Steak

Start to Finish: 30 minutes Makes: 4 servings
- 2 12-ounce boneless beef top loin steaks, cut 1¼ inches thick
- 2 slices bacon
- ½ cup bottled balsamic vinaigrette salad dressing
- 8 slices tomato
- 2 cups mixed baby greens

1 Trim fat from steaks. For a charcoal grill, grill steaks on the rack of an uncovered grill directly over medium coals until desired doneness, turning once halfway through grilling. Allow 14 to 18 minutes for medium rare (145°F) and 18 to 22 minutes for medium (160°F). (For a gas grill, preheat grill. Reduce heat to medium. Place steaks on grill rack over heat. Cover; grill as above.)

2 Meanwhile, for sauce, in a large skillet cook bacon over medium heat until crisp. Remove bacon from skillet, reserving 1 tablespoon drippings in skillet. Drain bacon on paper towels. Crumble bacon; set aside. Add the salad dressing to the hot skillet. Cook and stir over high heat about 1 minute, scraping up browned bits in bottom of skillet. Remove skillet from heat.

3 To serve, halve each steak. Place a piece of steak on each of 4 dinner plates. Top each with 2 tomato slices, some of the crumbled bacon, and some of the mixed greens. Pour some of the sauce over each steak.

Nutrition Facts per serving: 556 cal., 42 g total fat (14 g sat. fat), 122 mg chol., 636 mg sodium, 5 g carbo., 1 g fiber, 38 g pro. Daily Values: 6% vit. A, 12% vit. C, 2% calcium, 17% iron

Steak with Tarragon Butter

0 net carbs

Start to Finish: 30 minutes Makes: 6 servings
- ¼ cup butter, softened
- 1 clove garlic, minced
- 1 teaspoon lemon juice
- ½ teaspoon dried tarragon, crushed
- 2 1-pound beef porterhouse, T-bone, or sirloin steaks, cut 1½ inches thick

1 For tarragon butter, in a small bowl stir together butter, garlic, lemon juice, and tarragon. Chill while preparing steaks.

2 Preheat broiler. Place steaks on the unheated rack of a broiler pan. Broil 4 to 5 inches from the heat until desired doneness, turning once halfway through broiling. Allow 20 to 25 minutes for medium rare (145°F) and 25 to 30 minutes for medium (160°F). Cut steaks into serving-size pieces. Serve with the tarragon butter.

Nutrition Facts per serving: 207 cal., 14 g total fat (7 g sat. fat), 64 mg chol., 128 mg sodium, 0 g carbo., 0 g fiber, 20 g pro. Daily Values: 6% vit. A, 1% vit. C, 2% calcium, 8% iron

Ribeyes with Creamy Onion Sauce

Prep: 10 minutes Broil: 12 minutes Makes: 4 servings
- 1 medium sweet onion (such as Maui or Walla Walla), thinly sliced
- 4 6-ounce boneless beef ribeye steaks, cut 1 inch thick
- 1 tablespoon Mediterranean seasoning blend or lemon-pepper seasoning
- 1 8-ounce container dairy sour cream
- 2 tablespoons capers, drained

1 Preheat broiler. Place onion slices on the rack of an unheated broiler pan. Broil 3 to 4 inches from heat for 5 minutes; turn onions over. Sprinkle both sides of steaks with 1½ teaspoons of the seasoning blend. Place steaks on the broiler pan rack with the onions. Broil steaks and onion about 5 minutes more or until onion is brown. Transfer onions to a cutting board. Continue broiling steaks to desired doneness, turning once halfway through broiling. Allow 7 to 9 minutes more for medium rare (145°F) or 10 to 13 minutes more for medium (160°F).

2 Meanwhile, for sauce, coarsely chop the cooked onion. In a small saucepan combine onion, sour cream, capers, and the remaining 1½ teaspoons seasoning blend. Cook and stir over medium-low heat until heated through (do not boil). Transfer steaks to 4 serving plates. Spoon some of the sauce over steaks. Pass remaining sauce.

Nutrition Facts per serving: 398 cal., 22 g total fat (11 g sat. fat), 106 mg chol., 472 mg sodium, 4 g carbo., 0 g fiber, 39 g pro.
Daily Values: 9% vit. A, 3% vit. C, 8% calcium, 17% iron

Olive-Stuffed Steaks

Pungent olives, capers, and garlic accent the hearty goodness of beef. Thick ribeye steaks are ideal for stuffing, but you also can use top loin or tenderloin steaks.

Prep: 20 minutes Grill: 22 minutes Makes: 4 servings

- ½ cup pimiento-stuffed green olives
- 1 tablespoon capers, drained
- 1½ teaspoons finely shredded orange peel
- ½ teaspoon black pepper
- 3 cloves garlic, chopped
- 2 beef ribeye steaks, cut 1¼ to 1½ inches thick

1 In a blender container or food processor bowl combine olives, capers, orange peel, pepper, and garlic. Cover and blend or process until mixture is chunky.

2 Trim fat from steaks. Cut each steak in half crosswise. Cut a horizontal pocket in each piece of steak by cutting from one side almost to, but not through, the other side. Spoon about 1 tablespoon of the olive mixture into each pocket. Spoon the remaining mixture over steaks; rub in with your fingers.

3 For a charcoal grill, arrange medium-hot coals around a drip pan. Test for medium heat above the pan. Place the steaks on grill rack directly over drip pan. Cover and grill until desired doneness. Allow 22 to 25 minutes for medium rare (145°F) and 25 to 28 minutes for medium (160°F). (For a gas grill, preheat grill. Reduce heat to medium. Adjust for indirect cooking. Grill as above.)

Nutrition Facts per serving: 278 cal., 13 g total fat (4 g sat. fat), 81 mg chol., 533 mg sodium, 2 g carbo., 0 g fiber, 38 g pro. Daily Values: 2% vit. A, 7% vit. C, 3% calcium, 19% iron

Prosciutto-Wrapped Beef

Prep: 15 minutes Broil: 12 minutes Makes: 4 servings
 1 ounce sliced prosciutto, chopped
 1 small carrot, shredded
 1 green onion, sliced
 4 beef tenderloin steaks, cut 1 inch thick
 4 thin slices prosciutto

1 For stuffing, combine the chopped prosciutto, carrot, and green onion. Cut a horizontal pocket in each steak by cutting from one side almost to, but not through, the other side. Fill pockets with stuffing. Cut the sliced prosciutto into 1-inch strips; wrap prosciutto strips around each steak. Secure with wooden toothpicks.

2 Preheat broiler. Place steaks on the unheated rack of a broiler pan. Broil 3 to 4 inches from the heat until desired doneness, turning once. Allow 12 to 14 minutes for medium rare (145°F) and 15 to 18 minutes for medium (160°F).

Nutrition Facts per serving: 296 cal., 13 g total fat (5 g sat. fat), 115 mg chol., 516 mg sodium, 1 g carbo., 0 g fiber, 40 g pro.
Daily Values: 51% vit. A, 2% vit. C, 2% calcium, 28% iron

Steak and Mushrooms

If you like, choose two or more varieties of the mushrooms to top these beef tenderloins.

Start to Finish: 20 minutes   Makes: 4 servings
- 4   beef tenderloin steaks, cut 1 inch thick (about 1 pound)
- 1   tablespoon olive oil
- 8   ounces crimini, shiitake, baby portobello, or button mushrooms, sliced (3 cups)
- ¼   cup seasoned beef broth
- ¼   cup whipping cream
    Salt and black pepper

1 In a large skillet cook steaks in hot oil over medium heat to desired doneness, turning once. Allow 7 to 9 minutes for medium rare (145°F) or 10 to 13 minutes for medium (160°F). Transfer steaks to a serving platter; keep warm.

2 In the same skillet cook and stir mushrooms for 4 to 5 minutes or until tender. Stir in broth and cream. Cook and stir over medium heat about 2 minutes or until slightly thickened. Season to taste with salt and black pepper. Spoon mushroom mixture over steaks.

Nutrition Facts per serving: 271 cal., 18 g total fat (7 g sat. fat), 90 mg chol., 116 mg sodium, 2 g carbo., 0 g fiber, 26 g pro.
Daily Values: 5% vit. A, 2% calcium, 19% iron

Teriyaki Beef Spirals

Score the steak with a sharp knife and pound it with a meat mallet to make it easier to roll into a spiral and more tender to eat.

Prep: 20 minutes Grill: 12 minutes Makes: 4 servings

- 1 cup loosely packed fresh spinach leaves
- ½ cup finely chopped water chestnuts
- ¼ cup chopped green onions (2)
- ¼ cup reduced-sodium teriyaki sauce
- ¾ to 1 pound beef flank steak
  - Salt and black pepper

1 Remove stems from spinach leaves. Layer leaves on top of each other; slice crosswise into thin strips. In a medium bowl combine spinach strips, water chestnuts, green onions, and 2 tablespoons of the teriyaki sauce.

2 Trim fat from steak. Score steak on both sides by making shallow cuts at 1-inch intervals in a diamond pattern. Place meat between 2 pieces of plastic wrap. Pound lightly with flat side of meat mallet into a 10×8-inch rectangle. Remove plastic wrap. Sprinkle steak with salt and pepper.

3 Spread spinach mixture over steak. Starting from a short side, roll steak up. Secure with wooden toothpicks at 1-inch intervals, starting ½ inch from one end. Slice between toothpicks into eight 1-inch slices. Thread 2 slices onto each of 4 long metal skewers. Brush slices with teriyaki sauce.

4 For a charcoal grill, grill slices on the rack of an uncovered grill directly over medium coals for 12 to 14 minutes for medium doneness, turning once and brushing with teriyaki sauce halfway through grilling. (For a gas grill, preheat grill. Reduce heat to medium. Place slices on grill rack over heat. Cover and grill as above.)

Nutrition Facts per serving: 135 cal., 6 g total fat (2 g sat. fat), 42 mg chol., 135 mg sodium, 2 g carbo., 1 g fiber, 18 g pro. Daily Values: 11% vit. A, 6% vit. C, 2% calcium, 11% iron

Zesty Grilled Sirloin

Marinate beef sirloin steak in a dried-chile-and-cumin paste overnight before grilling. The finished steak will be juicy and mouthwatering, with a flavor that's just right.

2 net carbs

Prep: 20 minutes Stand: 30 minutes Marinate: 24 hours Grill: 24 minutes
Makes: 12 servings

- 1½ ounces dried red chile peppers (7 or 8 chiles), such as guajillo, ancho, or pasilla
- 1 tablespoon ground cumin
- ½ cup olive oil
- 1 2¾- to 3-pound beef sirloin steak, cut 2 inches thick

1 Wearing plastic or rubber gloves, use a sharp knife to remove the stalk ends from the peppers. Split peppers; remove and discard seeds. In a heavy skillet, toast peppers (without oil) over medium heat for 3 to 4 minutes or until fragrant, turning once or twice with tongs. Transfer peppers to a small bowl. Cover with hot water and soak for 30 minutes. Drain, reserving 1 cup of the water. Place peppers in a blender or food processor. In the same skillet toast cumin over medium heat for 1 to 2 minutes or until fragrant, stirring often. Place cumin and olive oil in blender or food processor with peppers. Blend or process until nearly smooth, adding enough of the water the peppers were soaked in to make a medium-thick paste. Set aside.

2 Trim fat from meat. Place steak in a self-sealing plastic bag set in a shallow dish. Spread pepper paste on both sides of steak. Seal bag. Marinate in the refrigerator for 24 hours, turning bag occasionally.

3 Drain steak, reserving marinade. For charcoal grill, grill steak on rack of uncovered grill directly over medium coals for 24 to 30 minutes for medium (160°F), turning halfway through and brushing with reserved marinade during first half of grilling. (For a gas grill, preheat grill. Reduce heat to medium. Place steak on grill rack. Cover grill and grill as above.) Discard remaining marinade. To serve, thinly slice meat across the grain.

Nutrition Facts per serving: 233 cal., 14 g total fat (3 g sat. fat), 63 mg chol., 56 mg sodium, 3 g carbo., 1 g fiber, 23 g pro.
Daily Values: 19% vit. A, 2% vit. C, 1% calcium, 16% iron

Sirloin with Mustard and Chives

Another time, you can use the same tangy sour cream topping to enhance grilled salmon steaks.

Prep: 10 minutes Grill: 14 minutes Makes: 4 servings
- 4 boneless beef top sirloin steaks, cut 1 inch thick
- 2 teaspoons garlic-pepper seasoning
- ½ cup dairy sour cream
- 2 tablespoons Dijon-style mustard
- 1 tablespoon snipped fresh chives

1 Sprinkle both sides of steaks with 1½ teaspoons of the garlic-pepper seasoning. For a charcoal grill, grill steaks on the rack of an uncovered grill directly over medium coals to desired doneness, turning once halfway through grilling. Allow 14 to 18 minutes for medium rare (145°F) or 18 to 22 minutes for medium (160°F). (For a gas grill, preheat grill. Reduce heat to medium. Place steaks on grill rack over heat. Cover and grill as above.)

2 Meanwhile, in a small bowl combine sour cream, mustard, chives, and the remaining ½ teaspoon garlic-pepper seasoning. Spoon sour cream mixture on top of steaks.

Nutrition Facts per serving: 277 cal., 12 g total fat (5 g sat. fat), 114 mg chol., 619 mg sodium, 2 g carbo., 0 g fiber, 37 g pro. Daily Values: 5% vit. A, 1% vit. C, 5% calcium, 25% iron

Tenderloins with Rosemary and Port

Whipping cream and port wine guarantee a richly flavored sauce that drapes elegantly over pan-fried tenderloins.

3
net carbs

Start to Finish: 20 minutes Makes: 4 servings
- 4 4- to 5-ounce beef tenderloin steaks, cut ¾ inch thick
-    Salt
-    Coarsely ground black pepper
- 1 tablespoon olive oil or cooking oil
- 1½ teaspoons snipped fresh rosemary
- ⅓ cup port wine
- ⅓ cup water
- ¼ cup whipping cream

1 Sprinkle both sides of steaks with salt and pepper. Add oil to a large skillet. Heat skillet over medium-high heat. Add steaks. Reduce heat to medium and cook for 10 to 13 minutes or until desired doneness, turning steaks once halfway through cooking (145°F for medium rare or 160°F for medium). Transfer steaks to a serving platter; keep warm.

2 For sauce, add rosemary to drippings in skillet. Cook and stir for 1 minute to loosen any brown bits in bottom of skillet. Carefully stir port and water into skillet. Bring to boiling. Boil, uncovered, about 3 minutes or until mixture is reduced by half. Stir in whipping cream. Return to boiling; boil gently for 2 to 3 minutes or until slightly thickened. Spoon sauce over steaks.

Nutrition Facts per serving: 295 cal., 18 g total fat (7 g sat. fat), 90 mg chol., 132 mg sodium, 3 g carbo., 0 g fiber, 24 g pro.
Daily Values: 5% vit. A, 2% calcium, 19% iron

8
net carbs

Sweet-Hot Pepper Steak

A combination of fiery jalapeños and sweet peppers tops these sirloin steaks. Use one green and one yellow or red sweet pepper for a more enticing look.

Start to Finish: 25 minutes Makes: 4 servings
- 1 pound boneless beef top sirloin steak, cut ¾ inch thick
   Salt and black pepper
   Nonstick cooking spray
- 2 medium yellow, green, and/or red sweet peppers, cut into thin strips
- 2 fresh jalapeño chile peppers, seeded and finely chopped*
- 1 medium onion, thinly sliced
- 2 cloves garlic, minced

1 Trim fat from meat. Sprinkle meat with salt and pepper. Lightly coat a large nonstick skillet with cooking spray. Heat skillet over medium-high heat. Add steak. Reduce heat to medium and cook for 10 to 13 minutes, turning steak halfway through cooking (145° for medium rare or 160°F for medium). Remove steak from skillet, reserving drippings in skillet. Cover steak; keep warm.

2 Add sweet pepper strips, chile peppers, onion, and garlic to drippings in skillet. Cook over medium heat about 5 minutes or until vegetables are crisp-tender, stirring occasionally. To serve, cut steak into 4 serving-size pieces. Top with pepper mixture.

*Note: Because hot chile peppers, such as jalapeños, contain volatile oils that can burn your skin and eyes, avoid direct contact with chiles as much as possible. When working with chile peppers, wear plastic or rubber gloves. If your bare hands do touch chile peppers, wash your hands well with soap and water.

Nutrition Facts per serving: 175 cal., 4 g total fat (1 g sat. fat), 69 mg chol., 131 mg sodium, 9 g carbo., 1 g fiber, 25 g pro.
Daily Values: 5% vit. A, 250% vit. C, 3% calcium, 19% iron

Spice-Rubbed Ribeyes

Prep: 5 minutes Grill: 11 minutes Makes: 4 servings
- 4 teaspoons chili powder
- 1 teaspoon ground coriander
- 1 teaspoon cumin seeds
- ½ teaspoon black pepper
- 4 6-ounce boneless beef ribeye steaks, cut 1 inch thick

1 For spice rub, in a small nonstick skillet cook and stir chili powder, coriander, cumin seeds, and pepper over medium heat for 1 minute; cool. Using your fingers, rub spice mixture onto both sides of steaks.

2 For a charcoal grill, grill steaks on the rack of an uncovered grill directly over medium coals until desired doneness, turning once halfway through grilling. Allow 11 to 15 minutes for medium rare (145°F) and 14 to 18 minutes for medium (160°F). (For a gas grill, preheat grill. Reduce heat to medium. Place steaks on grill rack over heat. Cover and grill as above.)

Nutrition Facts per serving: 267 cal., 11 g total fat (4 g sat. fat), 81 mg chol., 115 mg sodium, 2 g carbo., 1 g fiber, 38 g pro.
Daily Values: 18% vit. A, 3% vit. C, 3% calcium, 20% iron

Caesar Beef-Vegetable Kabobs

These kabobs are named after the Caesar salad dressing that is used as a marinade. The meat and veggie combo, however, is equally tasty when marinated in Italian salad dressing.

Prep: 30 minutes Marinate: 2 hours Grill: 12 minutes Makes: 4 servings

- 1 pound boneless beef sirloin steak, cut 1 inch thick
- 8 cherry tomatoes
- 8 whole fresh button mushrooms
- 1 large yellow or green sweet pepper, cut into 1-inch pieces
- ½ cup bottled Caesar salad dressing
- ½ teaspoon black pepper

1 Cut steak into 1-inch cubes. Place steak cubes, tomatoes, mushrooms, and sweet pepper in a self-sealing plastic bag set in a shallow dish.

2 For marinade, combine salad dressing and black pepper. Pour over steak and vegetables; seal bag. Marinate in refrigerator for 2 to 4 hours, turning bag occasionally.

3 Remove steak and vegetables from the marinade; discard marinade. On eight 6- to 8-inch metal skewers, alternately thread steak, tomatoes, mushrooms, and sweet pepper pieces, leaving a ¼-inch space between the pieces.

4 For a charcoal grill, grill kabobs on the rack of an uncovered grill directly over medium coals for 12 to 14 minutes for medium doneness, turning once. (For a gas grill, preheat grill. Reduce heat to medium. Place kabobs on grill rack over heat. Cover and grill as above.)

Nutrition Facts per serving: 338 cal., 23 g total fat (4 g sat. fat), 69 mg chol., 385 mg sodium, 7 g carbo., 1 g fiber, 26 g pro. Daily Values: 6% vit. A, 133% vit. C, 2% calcium, 21% iron

Steak Skewers with Lemon Dipping Sauce

If using wooden skewers when making kabobs, soak them in water for at least 1 hour before threading the meat on them. Otherwise the wood may scorch when you grill the kabobs.

Prep: 30 minutes Marinate: 2 to 24 hours Grill: 10 minutes Makes: 4 servings
- 1   1- to 1¼-pound beef flank steak
- ⅓   cup bottled lemon-pepper marinade
- 1   medium lemon
- ⅓   cup dairy sour cream
- 1   teaspoon prepared horseradish

1 Trim fat from meat. Slice beef across the grain into thin slices. Place meat in a self-sealing plastic bag set in a medium bowl. Pour marinade over meat; seal bag. Marinate in refrigerator for 2 to 24 hours.

2 Meanwhile, for dipping sauce, finely shred 1 teaspoon peel from the lemon. Cut lemon in half; squeeze until you have 1 teaspoon juice. In a small bowl combine lemon peel, lemon juice, sour cream, and horseradish. Cover and chill at least 2 hours or up to 24 hours.

3 Thread steak slices accordion-style onto 10- to 12-inch metal skewers. For a charcoal grill, grill skewers on the rack of an uncovered grill directly over medium coals for 10 to 12 minutes or until desired doneness, turning occasionally. (For a gas grill, preheat grill. Reduce heat to medium. Place skewers on grill rack over heat. Cover and grill as above.) Serve skewers with dipping sauce.

Nutrition Facts per serving: 217 cal., 12 g total fat (5 g sat. fat), 63 mg chol., 611 mg sodium, 2 g carbo., 0 g fiber, 24 g pro. Daily Values: 3% vit. A, 3% vit. C, 3% calcium, 12% iron

Asian-Style Beef Soup

The seasoning from the packaged beef strips lends an extra layer of flavor, but don't worry if you choose to use leftover roast beef or beef from the deli. The fresh ginger tastes great on its own.

Start to Finish: 15 minutes   Makes: 4 servings

- 3 14-ounce cans beef broth
- 1 16-ounce package frozen loose-pack broccoli stir-fry vegetables
- 3 tablespoons teriyaki sauce
- 2 teaspoons grated fresh ginger or ½ teaspoon ground ginger
- 1 9-ounce package frozen cooked seasoned beef strips, thawed and cut up, or 2 cups chopped cooked beef

1 In a large saucepan bring beef broth to boiling. Stir in frozen vegetables, teriyaki sauce, and ginger. Return to boiling; reduce heat. Simmer, covered, for 3 to 5 minutes or until vegetables are tender. Stir in beef strips; heat through.

Nutrition Facts per serving: 177 cal., 6 g total fat (2 g sat. fat), 41 mg chol., 1,885 mg sodium, 10 g carbo., 2 g fiber, 21 g pro.
Daily Values: 30% vit. A, 41% vit. C, 11% iron

Pecan Pork Chops

Start to Finish: 15 minutes Makes: 4 servings
- 4 boneless pork loin chops, cut ¾ inch thick
   Salt and black pepper
- ¼ cup butter, softened
- 2 tablespoons reduced-calorie maple-flavor syrup
- ⅓ cup chopped toasted pecans

1 Trim fat from chops. Sprinkle both sides of chops with salt and pepper. In a 12-inch skillet cook chops in 1 tablespoon of the butter over medium-high heat for 9 to 13 minutes or until done (160°F), turning once. Transfer chops to a serving platter; keep warm.

2 Meanwhile, in a small bowl combine the remaining 3 tablespoons butter and the maple syrup. Spread butter mixture evenly over chops. Let stand about 1 minute or until melted. Sprinkle with pecans.

Nutrition Facts per serving: 319 cal., 23 g total fat (10 g sat. fat), 98 mg chol., 324 mg sodium, 5 g carbo., 1 g fiber, 23 g pro. Daily Values: 9% vit. A, 1% vit. C, 2% calcium, 6% iron

5
net carbs

Country Chops and Peppers

Start to Finish: 20 minutes Makes: 4 servings

- 4 pork loin chops, cut ¾ inch thick
  Seasoned salt and black pepper
  Nonstick cooking spray
- 1 medium sweet pepper, cut into strips
- 1 tablespoon butter
- ⅓ cup white wine Worcestershire sauce or 2 tablespoons Worcestershire sauce and ¼ cup water

1 Trim fat from chops. Sprinkle chops on both sides with seasoned salt and black pepper. Lightly coat a large skillet with cooking spray. Heat skillet over medium-high heat. Add chops. Cook for 5 minutes. Turn chops; top with sweet pepper strips. Cover and cook for 5 to 7 minutes more or until chops are done (160°F) and sweet pepper strips are crisp-tender. Remove chops and sweet pepper strips from skillet; keep warm.

2 For sauce, add butter and Worcestershire sauce to hot skillet. Cook over medium heat until mixture thickens slightly, stirring constantly to loosen any brown bits in bottom of skillet. Pour sauce over chops and sweet pepper strips.

Nutrition Facts per serving: 282 cal., 11 g total fat (5 g sat. fat), 101 mg chol., 282 mg sodium, 6 g carbo., 1 g fiber, 38 g pro.
Daily Values: 6% vit. A, 38% vit. C, 6% calcium, 9% iron

Beer-Glazed Pork Chops

Prep: 15 minutes Marinate: 6 to 24 hours Grill: 30 minutes Makes: 4 servings
- 4 boneless pork top loin chops, cut 1¼ to 1½ inches thick
- 1 12-ounce bottle stout (dark beer)
- ¼ cup honey mustard
- 1 teaspoon caraway seeds
- 3 cloves garlic, minced

1 Trim fat from chops. Place chops in a self-sealing plastic bag set in a shallow dish. For marinade, stir together stout, mustard, caraway seeds, and garlic. Pour over chops; seal bag. Marinate in refrigerator for 6 to 24 hours, turning bag occasionally.

2 Drain chops; pour marinade into a small saucepan. Bring to boiling; reduce heat. Simmer, uncovered, about 15 minutes or until marinade is reduced by about half.

3 For a charcoal grill, arrange medium-hot coals around a drip pan. Test for medium heat above the pan. Place chops on grill rack over drip pan. Cover and grill for 30 to 35 minutes or until done (160°F), brushing frequently with marinade during the last 10 minutes of grilling. (For a gas grill, preheat grill. Reduce heat to medium. Adjust for indirect cooking. Grill as above.) Discard any remaining marinade.

Nutrition Facts per serving: 328 cal., 11 g total fat (4 g sat. fat), 108 mg chol., 90 mg sodium, 5 g carbo., 0 g fiber, 44 g pro.
Daily Values: 1% vit. C, 1% calcium, 7% iron

2 net carbs

Lemon and Herb-Rubbed Pork Chops

Prep: 15 minutes Grill: 35 minutes Makes: 4 servings

    4 teaspoons bottled minced garlic
 1½ teaspoons finely shredded lemon peel
    1 teaspoon dried rosemary, crushed
  ½ teaspoon salt
  ½ teaspoon black pepper
  ½ teaspoon dried sage, crushed
    4 pork loin chops, cut 1¼ inches thick

1 Trim fat from chops. For rub, combine garlic, lemon peel, rosemary, salt, pepper, and sage. Using your fingers, rub mixture onto both sides of chops.

2 For a charcoal grill, arrange medium-hot coals around a drip pan. Test for medium heat above drip pan. Place chops on grill rack directly over drip pan. Cover and grill for 35 to 40 minutes or until done (160°F), turning once halfway through grilling. (For a gas grill, preheat grill. Reduce heat to medium. Adjust for indirect cooking. Grill as above.)

Nutrition Facts per serving: 292 cal., 10 g total fat (4 g sat. fat), 105 mg chol., 371 mg sodium, 3 g carbo., 1 g fiber, 43 g pro.
Daily Values: 1% vit. A, 6% vit. C, 5% calcium, 8% iron

Pork Chops Dijon

2
net carbs

Start to Finish: 30 minutes Makes: 4 servings
- 3 tablespoons Dijon-style mustard
- 2 tablespoons bottled Italian salad dressing
- ¼ teaspoon black pepper
- 4 pork loin chops, cut ½ inch thick
  Nonstick cooking spray
- 1 medium onion, halved and sliced

1 In a small bowl combine mustard, salad dressing, and pepper; set aside. Trim fat from chops. Lightly coat a large skillet with cooking spray. Heat skillet over medium-high heat. Add chops to skillet; brown on both sides. Remove chops from skillet.

2 Add onion to skillet. Cook and stir over medium heat for 3 minutes. Push onion aside; return chops to skillet. Spread mustard mixture over chops. Cook, covered, over medium-low heat about 15 minutes or until done (160°F). Serve onion over chops.

Nutrition Facts per serving: 249 cal., 11 g total fat (3 g sat. fat), 88 mg chol., 382 mg sodium, 3 g carbo., 1 g fiber, 30 g pro.
Daily Values: 4% vit. C, 2% calcium, 6% iron

6
net carbs

Pork Chop Skillet for Two

A pair of chops is the ideal dinner when the kids are away; double the recipe and invite a couple of your best friends to join you.

Start to Finish: 40 minutes Makes: 2 servings
- 2 pork loin or rib chops, cut 1¼ to 1½ inches thick
- ¼ teaspoon coarsely ground black pepper
- ⅛ teaspoon salt
- 1 tablespoon cooking oil
- 1 cup baby summer squash (such as green or yellow pattypan and zucchini)
- ¾ cup half-and-half or light cream
- ½ teaspoon coriander seeds, coarsely crushed

1 Trim fat from chops. Sprinkle chops with pepper and salt. In a large skillet heat oil over medium heat. Add chops to skillet. Cook, uncovered, for 18 to 20 minutes or until done (160°F), turning once.

2 Meanwhile, if necessary, cut larger squash pieces into slices or halves. Add squash to skillet during the last 5 minutes of cooking. Remove chops and squash from skillet; keep warm.

3 Drain fat from skillet. For sauce, add half-and-half and coriander to hot skillet, stirring to loosen any brown bits in bottom of skillet. Bring to boiling; reduce heat. Simmer, uncovered, 5 to 7 minutes or until sauce is slightly thickened and reduced to about ¼ cup. Spoon sauce over chops.

Nutrition Facts per serving: 758 cal., 44 g total fat (17 g sat. fat), 254 mg chol., 388 mg sodium, 8 g carbo., 2 g fiber, 76 g pro.
Daily Values: 13% vit. A, 13% vit. C, 18% calcium, 18% iron

Orange-Marinated Pork Chops

Bottled minced garlic is a real timesaver, but feel free to use cloves of fresh garlic. One clove equals ½ teaspoon minced garlic.

Prep: 15 minutes Marinate: 4 to 12 hours Grill: 12 minutes Makes: 4 servings

- 4 boneless pork loin chops, cut ¾ inch thick
- 1 orange
- ½ cup chicken broth
- 2 tablespoons reduced-sodium soy sauce
- 1 teaspoon bottled minced garlic

1 Trim fat from chops. Place chops in a self-sealing plastic bag set in a shallow dish. Finely shred 1 tablespoon peel from orange. Cut orange in half; squeeze orange until you have ¼ cup juice. For marinade, in a small bowl combine the orange peel, orange juice, chicken broth, soy sauce, and garlic. Pour over chops; seal bag. Marinate in refrigerator 4 to 12 hours, turning bag occasionally.

2 Drain chops, discarding marinade. For a charcoal grill, grill chops on the rack of an uncovered grill directly over medium coals for 12 to 15 minutes or until done (160°F), turning once. (For a gas grill, preheat grill. Reduce heat to medium. Place chops on grill rack over heat. Cover and grill as above.)

Nutrition Facts per serving: 253 cal., 10 g total fat (3 g sat. fat), 92 mg chol., 137 mg sodium, 1 g carbo., 0 g fiber, 37 g pro. Daily Values: 4% vit. C, 1% calcium, 6% iron

Spicy Orange-Glazed Pork Chops

Prep: 10 minutes Grill: 12 minutes Makes: 4 servings
- ¼ cup sugar-free or low-sugar orange marmalade
- 2 teaspoons Dijon-style mustard
- 1 teaspoon lemon juice
- ⅛ to ¼ teaspoon cayenne pepper
- 4 boneless pork loin chops, cut ¾ inch thick
  Salt and black pepper

1 For glaze, in a small bowl stir together orange marmalade, mustard, lemon juice, and cayenne pepper. Set glaze aside.

2 Trim fat from chops. Sprinkle chops with salt and black pepper. For a charcoal grill, grill chops on the greased rack of an uncovered grill directly over medium coals for 12 to 15 minutes or until done (160°F), turning once and brushing frequently with glaze during the last few minutes of grilling. (For a gas grill, preheat grill. Reduce heat to medium. Place chops on greased grill rack over heat. Cover and grill as above.)

Nutrition Facts per serving: 263 cal., 10 g total fat (3 g sat. fat), 92 mg chol., 126 mg sodium, 5 g carbo., 0 g fiber, 37 g pro. Daily Values: 1% vit. A, 2% vit. C, 1% calcium, 6% iron

Paprika Pork Chops

Prep: 10 minutes Broil: 9 minutes Makes: 4 servings
- 2   teaspoons paprika
- 1   teaspoon garlic salt
- ½   teaspoon black pepper
- 4   pork loin chops, cut ¾ inch thick
- ½   cup dairy sour cream

1 In a small bowl stir together paprika, garlic salt, and pepper. Trim fat from chops. Using your fingers, rub the paprika mixture onto both sides of chops.

2 Preheat broiler. Place chops on the unheated rack of a broiler pan. Broil 3 to 4 inches from heat for 9 to 12 minutes or until done (160°F), turning once halfway through broiling. Serve with sour cream.

Nutrition Facts per serving: 246 cal., 12 g total fat (5 g sat. fat), 87 mg chol., 310 mg sodium, 2 g carbo., 0 g fiber, 31 g pro.
Daily Values: 17% vit. A, 2% vit. C, 5% calcium, 7% iron

Spanish-Style Pork Chops

If you need to make these stuffed chops ahead of time, no problem. After you've stuffed them, cover the chops with foil or plastic wrap and refrigerate them for up to 4 hours. Continue as directed.

Prep: 20 minutes Cook: 18 minutes Makes: 4 servings

- ⅓ cup shredded Monterey Jack cheese
- ½ cup pimiento-stuffed green olives, finely chopped
- 4 boneless pork top loin chops, cut 1¼ inches thick (about 1¾ pounds total)
- ½ teaspoon black pepper
- 1 tablespoon olive oil
- ¼ cup chicken broth
- ¼ cup chopped tomato
- 1 tablespoon snipped fresh parsley

1 For filling, in a small bowl combine the cheese and ¼ cup of the olives; set aside.

2 Trim fat from chops. Cut a horizontal pocket in each chop by cutting from the fatty side almost to, but not through, the other side. Divide filling among pockets in chops. If necessary, secure pockets with wooden toothpicks. Sprinkle chops with pepper.

3 In a large skillet heat oil over medium-high heat. Add chops; cook for 8 to 10 minutes or until brown, turning once.

4 Carefully pour broth over chops. Bring to boiling; reduce heat. Simmer, covered, about 10 minutes or until done (160°F). Meanwhile, in a small bowl combine the remaining ¼ cup olives, the tomato, and parsley. To serve, remove toothpicks from chops; top with tomato mixture.

Nutrition Facts per serving: 369 cal., 19 g total fat (6 g sat. fat), 118 mg chol., 614 mg sodium, 1 g carbo., 0 g fiber, 46 g pro.
Daily Values: 5% vit. A, 5% vit. C, 13% calcium, 11% iron

Greek-Style Pork Chops

Crumbled feta and chopped fresh tomato make a colorful topping for grilled chops. A garnish of snipped oregano enhances the bold Greek flavors.

Prep: 15 minutes Grill: 12 minutes Makes: 4 servings
- 1 small tomato, seeded and chopped (½ cup)
- 1 tablespoon bottled red wine vinaigrette salad dressing
- 4 boneless pork loin chops, cut ¾ inch thick
- 1 teaspoon lemon-pepper seasoning
- ¼ cup crumbled feta cheese with garlic and herb
   Snipped fresh oregano (optional)

1 In a small bowl stir together tomato and salad dressing. Set aside. Trim fat from chops. Rub lemon-pepper seasoning on both sides of chops. For a charcoal grill, grill chops on the rack of an uncovered grill directly over medium coals for 12 to 15 minutes or until done (160°F), turning once. (For a gas grill, preheat grill. Reduce heat to medium. Place chops on grill rack over heat. Cover and grill as above.)

2 Transfer chops to serving plates. Top each chop with some of the feta cheese and some of the tomato mixture. If desired, sprinkle each serving with oregano.

Nutrition Facts per serving: 179 cal., 7 g total fat (3 g sat. fat), 80 mg chol., 298 mg sodium, 3 g carbo., 0 g fiber, 25 g pro.
Daily Values: 4% vit. A, 9% vit. C, 6% calcium, 6% iron

Pork with Apple Brandy and Cream

Start to Finish: 25 minutes Makes: 4 servings
- 1 12-ounce pork tenderloin
- 2 tablespoons butter
- ½ cup whipping cream
- 1 2½-ounce can whole mushrooms, drained
- 2 tablespoons Calvados, apple jack, brandy, or apple juice

1 Cut tenderloin crosswise into 1-inch slices. Place each slice between 2 pieces of plastic wrap. Pound lightly with the flat side of a meat mallet to ½-inch thickness. Remove plastic wrap.

2 In a large skillet cook half the pork at a time in hot butter over medium heat for 5 to 6 minutes or until done (160°F), turning once. Transfer meat to a serving plate; keep warm.

3 For sauce, add whipping cream, mushrooms, and Calvados to hot skillet, stirring to loosen any brown bits in bottom of skillet. Bring to boiling; reduce heat. Simmer for 3 to 5 minutes or until slightly thickened. Pour sauce over meat.

Nutrition Facts per serving: 279 cal., 20 g total fat (12 g sat. fat), 112 mg chol., 183 mg sodium, 2 g carbo., 0 g fiber, 19 g pro.
Daily Values: 13% vit. A, 1% vit. C, 3% calcium, 7% iron

Soy and Sesame Pork

To toast sesame seeds, spread them in a single layer in a shallow baking pan and bake in a 350°F oven about 5 minutes or until light golden brown, watching carefully and stirring once or twice so they don't burn.

Prep: 5 minutes Marinate: 4 to 24 hours Roast: 20 minutes Oven: 425°F
Makes: 4 servings

- 1 1-pound pork tenderloin
- ¼ cup reduced-sodium soy sauce
- 1 tablespoon catsup
- ¼ teaspoon garlic powder
- 2 to 3 tablespoons toasted sesame seeds

1 Trim fat from pork. Place pork in a self-sealing plastic bag set in a shallow dish. For marinade, in a small bowl combine soy sauce, catsup, and garlic powder. Pour over pork; seal bag. Marinate in the refrigerator for 4 to 24 hours, turning bag occasionally.

2 Drain pork, discarding marinade. Place pork on a rack in a shallow roasting pan. Roast in a 425° oven for 20 to 30 minutes or until done (160°F). Sprinkle sesame seeds on a piece of foil; carefully roll pork in sesame seeds.

Nutrition Facts per serving: 162 cal., 5 g total fat (1 g sat. fat), 73 mg chol., 357 mg sodium, 2 g carbo., 1 g fiber, 25 g pro.
Daily Values: 1% vit. A, 2% vit. C, 2% calcium, 10% iron

Macadamia Nut-Crusted Pork

Start to Finish: 35 minutes Makes: 4 servings
- ¼ cup butter
- 1 12-ounce pork tenderloin
- 1 3½-ounce jar (about 1 cup) macadamia nuts
- ¼ teaspoon salt
- ¼ teaspoon black pepper

1 For clarified butter, in a small heavy saucepan, melt butter over low heat without stirring. When butter is completely melted, slowly pour the clear, oily layer into a custard cup, leaving the milky layer in the pan. The clear liquid is the clarified butter (you should have about 3 tablespoons). Discard the milky portion.

2 Cut pork tenderloin crosswise into 4 slices. Place each slice between 2 pieces of plastic wrap. Pound lightly with the flat side of a meat mallet to ¼-inch thickness. Remove plastic wrap. Set pork aside.

3 Place nuts in a food processor or blender. Cover and process or blend until chopped. In a small bowl combine chopped nuts, salt, and pepper. Lightly brush the surface of each tenderloin slice with about half of the clarified butter. Sprinkle nut mixture over each tenderloin slice, firmly pressing into both sides so nuts stick to the meat.

4 In a large skillet heat the remaining clarified butter over medium-high heat. Cook half the pork at a time in hot butter over medium heat for 5 to 6 minutes or until done (160°F), turning once.

Nutrition Facts per serving: 439 cal., 40 g total fat (12 g sat. fat), 83 mg chol., 385 mg sodium, 4 g carbo., 3 g fiber, 19 g pro. Daily Values: 9% vit. A, 1% vit. C, 3% calcium, 11% iron

Pork Medallions on Green Beans

It's easier to slice the pork when slightly frozen. Put it in the freezer for an hour or until partially frozen.

Start to Finish: 20 minutes Makes: 4 servings
- 1 1- to 1½-pound honey-mustard marinated pork tenderloin
- 1 tablespoon butter
- 1 9-ounce package frozen French-cut green beans, thawed
- 1 teaspoon dried dill
- 1 teaspoon lemon juice

1 Cut tenderloin into ¼-inch slices. In a 12-inch skillet cook pork in hot butter over medium heat 4 to 6 minutes or until done (160°F), turning once. Remove pork from skillet, reserving drippings in skillet. Keep warm.

2 Add green beans and dill to drippings in skillet. Cook and stir for 3 to 4 minutes or until beans are tender. Stir in lemon juice. Transfer beans to a serving platter. Serve pork medallions on top of green beans.

Nutrition Facts per serving: 187 cal., 8 g total fat (4 g sat. fat), 53 mg chol., 549 mg sodium, 7 g carbo., 2 g fiber, 21 g pro.
Daily Values: 9% vit. A, 3% vit. C, 2% calcium, 6% iron

Barbecued Baby Back Ribs

A combination of spices, sage, and celery seeds along with a brush of apple juice ensures moist, juicy, and flavorful ribs. Pictured on the front cover.

Prep: 15 minutes Grill: 1¼ hours Makes: 8 servings

    3½ to 4 pounds pork loin back ribs
      1 tablespoon paprika
    1½ teaspoons garlic salt
      1 teaspoon onion powder
      1 teaspoon dried sage, crushed
      ½ teaspoon celery seeds
      ¼ teaspoon cayenne pepper
      ½ cup apple juice

1 Trim fat from ribs. In a small bowl stir together paprika, garlic salt, onion powder, sage, celery seeds, and cayenne pepper. Rub spice mixture over both sides of ribs.

2 For a charcoal grill, arrange medium-hot coals around a drip pan. Test for medium heat above the drip pan. Place ribs on grill rack over drip pan. Cover and grill for 1¼ to 1½ hours or until ribs are tender, brushing occasionally with apple juice after the first 45 minutes of grilling. (For a gas grill, preheat grill. Adjust for indirect cooking. Grill as above.)

Nutrition Facts per serving: 207 cal., 8 g total fat (5 g sat. fat), 59 mg chol., 232 mg sodium, 3 g carbo., 0 g fiber, 27 g pro. Daily Values: 8% vit. A, 1% vit. C, 2% calcium, 6% iron

6 net carbs

Prep: 20 minutes   Grill: 50 minutes   Stand: 15 minutes   Makes: 4 servings

- 1   2½-pound lamb rib roast (8 ribs)
- ¼   cup purchased basil pesto
- 2   tablespoons finely chopped toasted hazelnuts (filberts) or walnuts
- ½   cup dairy sour cream
- 2   tablespoons purchased basil pesto

1 Trim fat from meat. In a small bowl stir together the ¼ cup pesto and the nuts. Spread over meat. Insert a meat thermometer into meat without touching bone.

2 For a charcoal grill, arrange medium-hot coals around a drip pan. Test for medium heat above the pan. Place meat, bone side down, on grill rack over drip pan. Cover and grill until desired doneness. Allow 50 to 60 minutes for medium rare (140°F) and 1 to 1½ hours for medium (155°F). (For a gas grill, preheat grill. Reduce heat to medium. Adjust for indirect cooking. Place meat, bone side down, in a roasting pan, place on grill rack, and grill as above.) Remove meat from grill. Cover meat with foil; let stand for 15 minutes. (The temperature of the meat will rise 5°F after standing.)

3 Meanwhile, for sauce, in a small bowl stir together sour cream and the 2 tablespoons pesto. To serve, cut meat into four 2-rib portions. Serve with sauce.

Nutrition Facts per serving: 441 cal., 33 g total fat (7 g sat. fat), 94 mg chol., 261 mg sodium, 6 g carbo., 0 g fiber, 29 g pro.
Daily Values: 4% vit. A, 1% vit. C, 5% calcium, 12% iron

Grilled Fennel-Cumin Lamb Chops

You can make the spice rub ahead of time and store it in an airtight container for up to 1 week.

Prep: 5 minutes Marinate: 1 to 24 hours Grill: 12 minutes Makes: 2 servings

- ¾ teaspoon fennel seeds, crushed
- ¾ teaspoon ground cumin
- ¼ teaspoon ground coriander
- ¼ teaspoon salt
- ⅛ teaspoon black pepper
- 1 clove garlic, minced
- 4 lamb rib chops, cut 1 inch thick

1 For spice rub, in a small bowl combine fennel seeds, cumin, coriander, salt, pepper, and garlic. Using your fingers, rub spice mixture onto both sides of chops. Place chops on a plate. Cover and chill for 1 to 24 hours.

2 For a charcoal grill, grill chops on the rack of an uncovered grill directly over medium coals to desired doneness, turning once. Allow 12 to 14 minutes for medium rare (145°F) and 15 to 17 minutes for medium (160°F). (For a gas grill, preheat grill. Reduce heat to medium. Place chops on grill rack over heat. Cover and grill as above.)

Nutrition Facts per serving: 248 cal., 14 g total fat (5 g sat. fat), 355 mg sodium, 1 g carbo., 0 g fiber, 29 g pro.
Daily Values: 39% calcium, 19% iron

Lamb Chops with Cilantro-Orange Butter

To scoop the flavored butter into balls, use a 1-teaspoon measuring spoon that has a round bowl.

Prep: 15 minutes Chill: 1 hour Grill: 12 minutes Makes: 4 servings
- ¼ cup butter, softened
- 2 tablespoons snipped fresh cilantro
- 1 teaspoon finely shredded orange peel
- 1 teaspoon bottled minced roasted garlic
- 8 lamb loin chops, cut 1 inch thick
- ¼ teaspoon salt
- ¼ teaspoon black pepper

1 In a small bowl combine butter, cilantro, orange peel, and garlic. Cover and chill at least 1 hour or until serving time.

2 Trim fat from chops. Sprinkle both sides of chops with salt and pepper. For a charcoal grill, grill chops on the rack of an uncovered grill directly over medium coals to desired doneness, turning once. Allow 12 to 14 minutes for medium rare (145°F) or 15 to 17 minutes for medium (160°F). (For a gas grill, preheat grill. Reduce heat to medium. Place chops on grill rack over heat. Cover and grill as above.) To serve, top each chop with some of the chilled butter mixture.

Nutrition Facts per serving: 281 cal., 19 g total fat (10 g sat. fat), 113 mg chol., 342 mg sodium, 1 g carbo., 0 g fiber, 26 g pro.
Daily Values: 12% vit. A, 3% vit. C, 2% calcium, 13% iron

Lamb Chops with Mint Marinade

Prep: 10 minutes **Marinate:** 1 to 24 hours **Grill:** 12 minutes **Makes:** 4 servings

- 8 lamb loin chops, cut 1 inch thick
- ¼ cup snipped fresh mint
- 2 tablespoons lemon juice
- 2 tablespoons olive oil
- ¼ teaspoon black pepper
- 3 cloves garlic, minced
- ¼ teaspoon salt

1 Trim fat from chops. Place chops in a self-sealing plastic bag set in a shallow dish. For marinade, combine 3 tablespoons of the mint, lemon juice, oil, pepper, and garlic. Pour over chops; seal bag. Marinate in refrigerator for 1 to 24 hours. Drain chops, discarding marinade. Sprinkle chops with salt.

2 For a charcoal grill, grill chops on the rack of an uncovered grill directly over medium coals to desired doneness, turning once. Allow 12 to 14 minutes for medium rare (145°F) and 15 to 17 minutes for medium (160°F). (For a gas grill, preheat grill. Reduce heat to medium. Place chops on grill rack over heat. Cover and grill as above.) Sprinkle chops with the remaining 1 tablespoon mint.

Nutrition Facts per serving: 310 cal., 18 g total fat (5 g sat. fat), 107 mg chol., 229 mg sodium, 2 g carbo., 0 g fiber, 34 g pro.
Daily Values: 1% vit. A, 12% vit. C, 2% calcium, 21% iron

chapter 2

Poultry

6

net carbs

Thai Chicken in Lettuce Cups

A sprinkle of chopped peanuts adds extra crunch to the spicy chicken strips and red onion nestled in lettuce leaves. The spiciness of this dish depends on the brand of Thai dressing used, so choose appropriately.

Start to Finish: 25 minutes Makes: 4 servings

- 12 ounces chicken breast tenders
- ¼ cup bottled Thai ginger salad dressing and marinade
- ½ cup thinly sliced red onion
- 4 Boston or Bibb lettuce cups
- 3 tablespoons coarsely chopped dry-roasted peanuts

1 In a medium bowl combine chicken and marinade; toss to coat. Let stand at room temperature for 10 minutes.

2 Heat a large skillet over medium-high heat for 2 minutes; add undrained chicken mixture and onion. Cook and stir for 3 to 5 minutes or until chicken is no longer pink and onion is tender. Divide chicken mixture among lettuce cups. Sprinkle with peanuts.

Nutrition Facts per serving: 156 cal., 5 g total fat (1 g sat. fat), 49 mg chol., 392 mg sodium, 6 g carbo., 0 g fiber, 22 g pro.
Daily Values: 3% vit. A, 5% vit. C, 2% calcium, 5% iron

Chicken Medallions with Mustard Sauce

For a company-pleasing presentation, spoon the sauce onto dinner plates, slice the chicken breasts, reassemble them on the sauce, and garnish with sprigs of fresh tarragon or dill.

Start to Finish: 25 minutes Makes: 4 servings

- 4 skinless, boneless chicken breast halves
  Salt and black pepper
- 2 tablespoons olive oil or cooking oil
- ¼ cup dry white wine
- 2 tablespoons crème fraîche
- 2 tablespoons tarragon mustard or dill mustard

1 Place each chicken breast half between 2 pieces of plastic wrap. Pound lightly with the flat side of a meat mallet to ½-inch thickness. Remove plastic wrap. Sprinkle chicken with salt and pepper.

2 In a 12-inch skillet cook chicken breasts, 2 at a time, in hot oil over medium-high heat for 2 to 3 minutes or until golden, turning once. Transfer chicken to a serving platter; keep warm.

3 For sauce, carefully add wine to hot skillet. Cook and stir until bubbly to loosen any brown bits in bottom of skillet. Add crème fraîche and mustard to skillet; stir with a wire whisk until combined. Spoon sauce over chicken.

Nutrition Facts per serving: 255 cal., 11 g total fat (3 g sat. fat), 92 mg chol., 306 mg sodium, 1 g carbo., 0 g fiber, 33 g pro.
Daily Values: 4% vit. A, 3% vit. C, 2% calcium, 6% iron

Stuffed Chicken Breasts

For extra zip, choose a flavored feta cheese for the stuffing.

Prep: 25 minutes Cook: 12 minutes Makes: 4 servings

- 4 skinless, boneless chicken breast halves
- 4 ounces crumbled feta cheese with peppercorn, feta cheese with garlic and herb, or plain feta cheese
- ½ of a 7-ounce jar roasted red sweet peppers, drained and cut into strips (½ cup)
- 1 tablespoon olive oil
- ¼ cup chicken broth

1 Place each chicken breast half between 2 pieces of plastic wrap. Pound lightly with the flat side of a meat mallet to ¼-inch thickness. Remove plastic wrap.

2 Sprinkle each chicken breast with cheese. Place sweet pepper strips in center of each breast. Fold narrow ends over filling; fold in sides. Roll up each breast half from a short side. Secure with wooden toothpicks.

3 In a medium nonstick skillet cook chicken in hot oil over medium heat about 5 minutes, turning to brown evenly. Add chicken broth. Bring to boiling; reduce heat. Simmer, covered, for 7 to 8 minutes or until chicken is no longer pink. To serve, spoon juices over chicken.

Nutrition Facts per serving: 265 cal., 11 g total fat (5 g sat. fat), 107 mg chol., 449 mg sodium, 2 g carbo., 0 g fiber, 37 g pro.
Daily Values: 3% vit. A, 77% vit. C, 15% calcium, 7% iron

Chicken Veronique

This version of the classic chicken and grape dish replaces the traditional cream sauce with a sauce of butter and sherry vinegar. If your grapes have seeds, halve them and remove the seeds with the tip of a spoon.

Start to Finish: 20 minutes Makes: 4 servings

- 4   skinless, boneless chicken breast halves
- ¼   teaspoon salt
- ¼   teaspoon black pepper
- ¼   cup butter
- 1   cup seedless red grapes, halved
- 3   tablespoons sherry vinegar or red wine vinegar
- ¼   teaspoon dried thyme, crushed

1 Sprinkle chicken with salt and pepper. In a large skillet cook chicken in 2 tablespoons of the hot butter over medium-high heat for 8 to 10 minutes or until no longer pink (170°F), turning once. Transfer to a serving platter; keep warm.

2 For sauce, add the remaining 2 tablespoons butter, grapes, vinegar, and thyme to hot skillet. Cook and stir until slightly thickened to loosen any brown bits in bottom of skillet. Serve sauce over chicken.

Nutrition Facts per serving: 301 cal., 15 g total fat (8 g sat. fat), 115 mg chol., 348 mg sodium, 7 g carbo., 0 g fiber, 33 g pro.
Daily Values: 11% vit. A, 10% vit. C, 3% calcium, 7% iron

Chicken and Pea Pods

Start to Finish: 25 minutes Makes: 4 servings
- 4 skinless, boneless chicken breast halves
- 2 teaspoons lemon-pepper seasoning
- 3 tablespoons butter
- 2 cups fresh sugar snap peas, strings and tips removed

1 Sprinkle both sides of chicken breasts with 1½ teaspoons of the lemon-pepper seasoning. In a large skillet cook chicken in 2 tablespoons of the hot butter over medium-high heat for 8 to 10 minutes or until chicken is no longer pink (170°F), turning once. Transfer chicken to a serving platter; keep warm.

2 Add remaining 1 tablespoon butter to skillet. Stir in pea pods and the remaining ½ teaspoon lemon-pepper seasoning. Cook and stir over medium heat for 2 to 3 minutes or until pea pods are crisp-tender. Serve the pea pods with the chicken.

Nutrition Facts per serving: 259 cal., 11 g total fat (6 g sat. fat), 107 mg chol., 716 mg sodium, 5 g carbo., 1 g fiber, 34 g pro. Daily Values: 27% vit. A, 19% vit. C, 6% calcium, 9% iron

Pesto Chicken with Summer Squash

Purchased pesto provides the burst of basil flavor. Look for jars of basil pesto near the spaghetti sauce in your supermarket.

Start to Finish: 20 minutes Makes: 4 servings

- 4 skinless, boneless chicken breast halves
- 1 tablespoon olive oil
- 2 cups finely chopped yellow summer squash or zucchini
- 2 tablespoons purchased basil pesto
- 2 tablespoons finely shredded Asiago or Parmesan cheese

1 In a large nonstick skillet cook chicken in hot oil over medium-high heat for 4 minutes.

2 Turn chicken; add squash to skillet. Cook for 4 to 6 minutes more or until chicken is no longer pink (170°F) and squash is crisp-tender, stirring squash gently once or twice. Transfer chicken and squash to 4 dinner plates. Spread pesto over chicken; sprinkle with cheese.

Nutrition Facts per serving: 186 cal., 10 g total fat (2 g sat. fat), 55 mg chol., 129 mg sodium, 2 g carbo., 1 g fiber, 23 g pro. Daily Values: 4% vit. A, 10% vit. C, 7% calcium, 5% iron

5
net carbs

Pepper and Peach Fajita Chicken

Start to Finish: 30 minutes Makes: 4 servings
    4 skinless, boneless chicken breast halves
 1½ teaspoons fajita seasoning
    2 tablespoons olive oil or butter
 1½ cups sweet pepper strips
    1 medium fresh peach or nectarine, cut into thin slices, or 1 cup frozen peach slices, thawed

1 Sprinkle both sides of chicken breast halves with fajita seasoning. In a large skillet cook chicken in 1 tablespoon of the hot oil over medium-high heat for 8 to 10 minutes or until chicken is no longer pink (170°F) turning once. Transfer chicken to a serving platter; keep warm.

2 Add remaining 1 tablespoon oil to skillet; add sweet pepper strips. Cook and stir about 3 minutes or until sweet pepper strips are crisp-tender. Gently stir in peach slices. Cook and stir for 1 to 2 minutes more or until heated through. Spoon over chicken.

Nutrition Facts per serving: 243 cal., 9 g total fat (1 g sat. fat), 82 mg chol., 150 mg sodium, 7 g carbo., 2 g fiber, 33 g pro.
Daily Values: 64% vit. A, 155% vit. C, 2% calcium, 7% iron

Crab-Stuffed Chicken

Prep: 25 minutes Cook: 25 minutes Makes: 4 servings
- 1 medium orange
- ½ of an 8-ounce tub cream cheese
- ⅛ teaspoon salt
- ⅛ teaspoon black pepper
- 1 6- to 6½-ounce can crabmeat, drained, flaked, and cartilage removed
- 4 medium skinless, boneless chicken breast halves
- 1 tablespoon butter

1 Finely shred 1 teaspoon peel from the orange. Cut orange in half; squeeze until you have 1 tablespoon juice. For filling, in a small bowl combine orange peel, orange juice, cream cheese, ⅛ teaspoon salt, and ⅛ teaspoon pepper. Gently stir in crabmeat; set filling aside.

2 Place each chicken breast half between 2 pieces of plastic wrap. Pound lightly with the flat side of a meat mallet into a rectangle about ⅛ inch thick. Remove plastic wrap. Sprinkle chicken with additional salt and pepper. Spread one-fourth of the filling evenly in center of each chicken piece. Fold narrow ends over filling; fold in sides. Roll up each chicken breast from a short side. Secure with wooden toothpicks.

3 In a medium skillet cook chicken in hot butter over medium-low heat 25 minutes or until no longer pink (170°F), turning to brown evenly.

Nutrition Facts per serving: 327 cal., 15 g total fat (9 g sat. fat), 161 mg chol., 467 mg sodium, 2 g carbo., 0 g fiber, 43 g pro.
Daily Values: 9% vit. A, 9% vit. C, 8% calcium, 8% iron

Cheesy Mediterranean Chicken

Prep: 20 minutes Cook: 25 minutes Makes: 4 servings
4 skinless, boneless chicken breast halves
   Salt and black pepper
4 oil-packed dried tomatoes, drained and cut into thin strips
2 ounces mascarpone cheese or crumbled feta cheese
4 teaspoons snipped fresh oregano, basil, tarragon, or parsley or ½ teaspoon dried oregano, basil, tarragon, or parsley, crushed
2 tablespoons olive oil

1 Place each chicken breast half between 2 pieces of plastic wrap. Pound lightly with the flat side of a meat mallet to ¼-inch thickness. Remove plastic wrap. Sprinkle chicken with salt and pepper.

2 On each breast, layer some of the tomato strips, cheese, and oregano. Fold narrow ends over filling; fold in sides. Roll up each breast half from a short side. Secure with wooden toothpicks.

3 In a medium skillet cook chicken in hot oil over medium-low heat about 25 minutes or until chicken is no longer pink (170°F), turning to brown evenly.

Nutrition Facts per serving: 257 cal., 17 g total fat (6 g sat. fat), 77 mg chol., 114 mg sodium, 2 g carbo., 0 g fiber, 25 g pro.
Daily Values: 1% vit. A, 11% vit. C, 1% calcium, 5% iron

Apple-Dijon Chicken

These butterflied chicken breasts cook in a flash in hot butter. Choose large chicken breast halves so you can butterfly them easily.

Start to Finish: 30 minutes Makes: 4 servings
- 4 large skinless, boneless chicken breast halves (about 1½ pounds)
  Salt and black pepper
- 2 tablespoons butter
- 1 medium tart cooking apple (such as Granny Smith), thinly sliced
- ⅓ cup whipping cream
- 2 tablespoons Dijon-style mustard

1 Butterfly cut each chicken breast half by cutting horizontally from one long side of the breast almost to, but not through, the opposite long side of the breast. Lay the breast open. Sprinkle both sides of chicken breasts with salt and pepper.

2 In a large skillet cook chicken, half at a time, in 1 tablespoon of the butter over medium-high heat until no longer pink (170°F), turning to brown evenly, about 2 to 3 minutes per side. Remove chicken from skillet; keep warm.

3 Add remaining 1 tablespoon butter to skillet. Add apple; cook and stir 3 minutes or until tender. Add whipping cream and mustard to skillet. Cook and stir until heated through and thickened slightly. Season to taste with additional salt and pepper. Serve sauce and apples over chicken.

Nutrition Facts per serving: 342 cal., 16 g total fat (9 g sat. fat), 142 mg chol., 407 mg sodium, 6 g carbo., 1 g fiber, 40 g pro. Daily Values: 11% vit. A, 6% vit. C, 4% calcium, 7% iron

net carbs

Easy Marinated Chicken Breasts

Widely used in Chinese cooking, hoisin sauce is thick, dark, and spicy. Stir it into marinades or pass it as a condiment for meat and poultry.

Prep: 10 minutes Marinate: 2 to 24 hours Grill: 12 minutes Makes: 8 servings

- 8 skinless, boneless chicken breast halves
- ½ cup bottled oil and vinegar salad dressing
- 3 tablespoons soy sauce
- 2 tablespoons bottled hoisin sauce
- ½ teaspoon ground ginger
  Bottled hoisin sauce (optional)

1 Place chicken breasts in a self-sealing plastic bag set in a shallow dish. For marinade, in a small bowl stir together the salad dressing, soy sauce, the 2 tablespoons hoisin sauce, and ginger. Pour over chicken; seal bag. Marinate in refrigerator for 2 to 24 hours, turning bag occasionally.

2 Drain chicken, discarding marinade. For a charcoal grill, grill chicken on the rack of an uncovered grill directly over medium coals for 12 to 15 minutes or until chicken is no longer pink (170°F). (For a gas grill, preheat grill. Reduce heat to medium. Place chicken on grill rack over heat. Cover and grill as above.) If desired, pass additional hoisin sauce for dipping.

Nutrition Facts per serving: 189 cal., 5 g total fat (1 g sat. fat), 82 mg chol., 286 mg sodium, 1 g carbo., 0 g fiber, 33 g pro.
Daily Values: 1% vit. A, 2% vit. C, 2% calcium, 5% iron

Chile-Lime Chicken Skewers

Prep: 20 minutes Grill: 10 minutes Makes: 4 servings
- 2 medium limes
- 1½ teaspoons ground ancho chile pepper
- 1 teaspoon garlic-herb seasoning
- 4 skinless, boneless chicken breast halves, cut into 1-inch strips

1 Finely shred lime peel from 1 lime until you have 1 teaspoon peel. Cut remaining lime into wedges; set wedges aside. In a small bowl combine lime peel, ground chile pepper, and garlic-herb seasoning. Using your fingers, rub lime mixture onto both sides of chicken strips.

2 Thread chicken strips accordion-style onto 4 long metal skewers. For a charcoal grill, grill skewers on the rack of an uncovered grill directly over medium coals for 10 to 12 minutes or until chicken is no longer pink, turning once. (For a gas grill, preheat grill. Reduce heat to medium. Place chicken on grill rack over heat. Cover and grill as above.) Serve skewers with lime wedges.

Nutrition Facts per serving: 132 cal., 2 g total fat (0 g sat. fat), 66 mg chol., 62 mg sodium, 1 g carbo., 0 g fiber, 26 g pro. Daily Values: 5% vit. A, 10% vit. C, 1% calcium, 4% iron

Chicken Breasts with Caper Vinaigrette

Capers and minced garlic freshen the flavor of bottled salad dressing. Another time, drizzle the versatile vinaigrette over grilled or broiled fish.

Prep: 15 minutes Grill: 12 minutes Makes: 4 servings

- ¼ cup oil-packed dried tomato strips
- 4 skinless, boneless chicken breast halves
- ¼ cup bottled Italian salad dressing
- 2 tablespoons capers, drained
- ¼ teaspoon black pepper
- 1 clove garlic, minced

1 Drain tomato strips, reserving oil. Set tomato strips aside. Brush chicken with some of the reserved oil.

2 For a charcoal grill, grill chicken on the rack of uncovered grill directly over medium coals for 12 to 15 minutes or until chicken is no longer pink (170°F), turning once and brushing with remaining reserved oil halfway through grilling. (For a gas grill, preheat grill. Reduce heat to medium. Place chicken on grill rack over heat. Cover and grill as above.)

3 Meanwhile, for vinaigrette, in a small bowl whisk together salad dressing, capers, pepper, and garlic.

4 Diagonally slice each chicken breast. Spoon vinaigrette over chicken. Top with tomato strips.

Nutrition Facts per serving: 218 cal., 4 g total fat (1 g sat. fat), 99 mg chol., 447 mg sodium, 3 g carbo., 1 g fiber, 40 g pro. Daily Values: 3% vit. A, 15% vit. C, 3% calcium, 8% iron

Cheesy Tuscan Chicken Pockets

Some skinless, boneless chicken breast halves are thicker than others. If possible, choose thick ones for this dish so it's easier to cut the pockets.

Prep: 15 minutes Grill: 12 minutes Makes: 4 servings
- 4 skinless, boneless chicken breast halves
- ¼ cup semisoft cheese with garlic and herb
- 3 to 4 ounces thinly sliced prosciutto
- ⅓ cup bottled Parmesan Italian salad dressing with basil

1 Using a sharp knife, cut a pocket in the side of each chicken breast half. Spread 1 tablespoon of the cheese in each pocket; top with a folded slice of prosciutto. Secure pockets with wooden toothpicks. Brush chicken with some of the salad dressing.

2 For a charcoal grill, grill chicken on the rack of uncovered grill directly over medium coals for 12 to 15 minutes or until chicken is no longer pink (170°F), turning once and brushing with remaining salad dressing halfway through grilling. (For a gas grill, preheat grill. Reduce heat to medium. Place chicken on grill rack over heat. Cover and grill as above.)

Nutrition Facts per serving: 312 cal., 15 g total fat (5 g sat. fat), 113 mg chol., 888 mg sodium, 2 g carbo., 0 g fiber, 40 g pro. Daily Values: 1% vit. A, 2% vit. C, 3% calcium, 6% iron

Italian Grilled Chicken

If you like, cut the grilled chicken into strips. Then serve it on a bed of greens and drizzle with additional dressing.

Prep: 10 minutes Marinate: 24 to 48 hours Grill: 12 minutes Makes: 8 servings
  8   skinless, boneless chicken breast halves
  ¾ cup bottled Italian salad dressing

1 Place chicken in a self-sealing plastic bag set in a large shallow dish. Pour salad dressing over chicken; seal bag. Marinate in refrigerator for 24 to 48 hours, turning bag occasionally.

2 Drain chicken, reserving marinade. For a charcoal grill, grill chicken on the rack of an uncovered grill directly over medium coals for 12 to 15 minutes or until chicken is no longer pink (170°F), turning once and brushing with reserved marinade halfway through grilling. (For a gas grill, preheat grill. Reduce heat to medium. Place chicken on grill rack over heat. Cover and grill as above.)

Nutrition Facts per serving: 232 cal., 12 g total fat (2 g sat. fat), 66 mg chol., 235 mg sodium, 2 g carbo., 0 g fiber, 26 g pro.
Daily Values: 1% vit. A, 2% vit. C, 2% calcium, 4% iron

Balsamic Chicken over Greens

Prep: 15 minutes Marinate: 1 to 4 hours Grill: 12 minutes Makes: 4 servings
- 4   skinless, boneless chicken breast halves
- 1   cup bottled balsamic vinaigrette salad dressing
- ¼   teaspoon crushed red pepper
- 3   cloves garlic, minced
- 8   cups torn mixed salad greens

1 Place chicken breast halves in a self-sealing plastic bag set in a shallow dish. For marinade, stir together ½ cup of the salad dressing, crushed red pepper, and garlic. Pour over chicken; seal bag. Marinate in the refrigerator for 1 to 4 hours, turning bag occasionally.

2 Drain chicken, reserving marinade. For a charcoal grill, grill chicken on the rack of an uncovered grill directly over medium coals for 12 to 15 minutes or until chicken is no longer pink (170°F), turning once and brushing with marinade halfway through grilling. (For a gas grill, preheat grill. Reduce heat to medium. Place chicken on grill rack over heat. Cover and grill as above.)

3 To serve, arrange greens on 4 serving plates. Cut chicken into strips; place on top of greens. Serve with the remaining ½ cup salad dressing.

Nutrition Facts per serving: 284 cal., 13 g total fat (2 g sat. fat), 82 mg chol., 525 mg sodium, 7 g carbo., 1 g fiber, 34 g pro. Daily Values: 21% vit. A, 14% vit. C, 6% calcium, 8% iron

2 net carbs

Tangy Lemon Chicken

Resist the temptation to brush the chicken with marinade after you have reached the halfway point of grilling to be sure any marinade on the chicken is cooked thoroughly. Discard remaining marinade after you turn the chicken.

Prep: 10 minutes Marinate: 2 to 4 hours Grill: 12 minutes Makes: 4 servings

- 4 medium skinless, boneless chicken breast halves (about 1 pound total)
- ½ cup bottled creamy Italian salad dressing
- 1 tablespoon finely shredded lemon peel
- ¼ cup lemon juice
  Dash black pepper
  Mixed salad greens (optional)

1 Place the chicken in a self-sealing plastic bag set in a shallow dish. For marinade, in a small bowl, stir together the salad dressing, lemon peel, lemon juice, and pepper. Pour over chicken. Seal bag. Marinate in the refrigerator for at least 2 hours or up to 4 hours, turning bag occasionally. Drain chicken, reserving marinade.

2 For a charcoal grill, grill chicken on the rack of an uncovered grill directly over medium coals for 12 to 15 minutes or until chicken is no longer pink (170°F), turning and brushing with marinade halfway through grilling. (For a gas grill, preheat grill. Reduce heat to medium. Place chicken on grill rack over heat. Cover and grill as above.) Discard any of remaining marinade. If desired, serve grilled chicken on salad greens.

Nutrition Facts per serving: 177 cal., 6 g total fat (1 g sat. fat), 66 mg chol., 179 mg sodium, 2 g carbo., 0 g fiber, 26 g pro.
Daily Values: 9% vit. C, 1% calcium, 5% iron

Mustard-Puff Chicken

Prep: 5 minutes Broil: 12 minutes Makes: 4 servings

- ⅓ cup mayonnaise
- 1 tablespoon Dijon-style mustard
- 1 tablespoon sliced green onion
- Dash cayenne pepper
- 4 skinless, boneless chicken breast halves

1 In a small bowl stir together the mayonnaise, mustard, green onion, and cayenne pepper. Set mayonnaise mixture aside.

2 Preheat broiler. Place chicken on the unheated rack of a broiler pan. Broil 4 to 5 inches from heat for 12 to 15 minutes or until no longer pink (170°F), turning once and brushing generously with mayonnaise mixture halfway through broiling.

Nutrition Facts per serving: 265 cal., 17 g total fat (2 g sat. fat), 72 mg chol., 182 mg sodium, 1 g carbo., 0 g fiber, 27 g pro.
Daily Values: 1% vit. A, 2% vit. C, 2% calcium, 5% iron

2
net carbs

Lemon-Dill Butter Chicken and Cucumbers

Take care not to overcook the cucumber. Cook just until it begins to soften and still has a bit of crispness. If you like, seed the cucumber before chopping it.

Prep: 10 minutes Broil: 12 minutes Makes: 4 servings

- 4 skinless, boneless chicken breast halves
- 1 medium lemon
- 3 tablespoons butter
- ½ teaspoon dried dill
- ¼ teaspoon salt
- ¼ teaspoon black pepper
- 1½ cups coarsely chopped cucumber or zucchini

1 Preheat broiler. Place chicken on the unheated rack of a broiler pan. Broil 4 to 5 inches from heat for 12 to 15 minutes or until no longer pink (170°F), turning once halfway through broiling.

2 Meanwhile, finely shred ½ teaspoon peel from the lemon. Cut lemon in half; squeeze lemon until you have 2 tablespoons juice.

3 In a small skillet melt butter over medium heat. Stir in lemon peel, lemon juice, dill, salt, and pepper. Stir in cucumber. Cook and stir over medium heat for 3 to 4 minutes or until cucumber is just tender. Spoon sauce over chicken.

Nutrition Facts per serving: 244 cal., 11 g total fat (6 g sat. fat), 107 mg chol., 477 mg sodium, 2 g carbo., 0 g fiber, 33 g pro.
Daily Values: 9% vit. A, 13% vit. C, 3% calcium, 7% iron

Florentine Chicken

Prep: 20 minutes Bake: 25 minutes Oven: 400°F Makes: 4 servings
- 1 12-ounce package frozen spinach soufflé
- 4 skinless, boneless chicken breast halves
- 1 4-ounce can sliced mushroom stems and pieces, drained
- ½ cup shredded cheddar cheese (2 ounces)

1 Run warm water over spinach soufflé for a few seconds to loosen. Remove soufflé from pan; divide into 4 squares. Place each chicken breast half between 2 pieces of plastic wrap. Pound lightly with the flat side of a meat mallet to ¼-inch thickness. Remove plastic wrap.

2 Place chicken pieces in a greased 3-quart rectangular baking dish. Top each piece with some of the mushrooms and 1 square of spinach soufflé. Bake, uncovered, in a 400° oven for 20 minutes. Sprinkle with cheese; bake about 5 minutes more or until chicken is no longer pink (170°F) and soufflé is heated through.

Nutrition Facts per serving: 331 cal., 14 g total fat (5 g sat. fat), 187 mg chol., 642 mg sodium, 8 g carbo., 1 g fiber, 41 g pro.
Daily Values: 30% vit. A, 4% vit. C, 20% calcium, 10% iron

6
net carbs

Baked Garlic Chicken

Prep: 20 minutes Bake: 45 minutes Oven: 325°F Makes: 6 servings

Nonstick cooking spray

2 to 2½ pounds meaty chicken pieces (breast halves, thighs, and drumsticks), skinned

25 cloves garlic (about ½ cup or 2 to 3 bulbs)

¼ cup dry white wine

Salt

Cayenne pepper

1 Lightly coat a large skillet with cooking spray. Heat skillet over medium heat. Add chicken; cook for 10 minutes, turning to brown evenly. Transfer chicken to a 2-quart square or rectangular baking dish. Add unpeeled garlic cloves and wine to baking dish. Sprinkle chicken with salt and cayenne pepper.

2 Bake, covered, in a 325° oven for 45 to 50 minutes or until chicken is no longer pink (170°F for breasts; 180°F for thighs and drumsticks).

Nutrition Facts per serving: 194 cal., 3 g total fat (1 g sat. fat), 96 mg chol., 232 mg sodium, 6 g carbo., 0 g fiber, 31 g pro.
Daily Values: 1% vit. A, 14% vit. C, 5% calcium, 8% iron

Three-Pepper Chicken

Most of the heat in chile peppers resides in the seeds. If you prefer your chicken spicy hot, do not seed the pepper. For a milder flavor, remove the seeds from the pepper.

Prep: 20 minutes Bake: 45 minutes Oven: 375°F Makes: 6 servings

- 2½ to 3 pounds meaty chicken pieces (breast halves, thighs, and drumsticks), skinned
- 3 tablespoons butter, melted
- 1 fresh jalapeño chile pepper, seeded and finely chopped*
- ¼ teaspoon salt
- ¼ teaspoon black pepper
- ¼ teaspoon cayenne pepper
- 4 cloves garlic, minced

1 Place chicken pieces, bone sides up, in a lightly greased 15×10×1-inch baking pan. Bake in a 375° oven for 25 minutes.

2 Meanwhile, in a small bowl stir together butter, chile pepper, salt, black pepper, cayenne pepper, and garlic. Brush some of the pepper mixture onto chicken. Turn chicken bone side down; brush with remaining pepper mixture. Bake 20 to 30 minutes more or until chicken is no longer pink (170°F for breasts; 180°F for thighs and drumsticks).

*Note: Because hot chile peppers, such as jalapeños, contain volatile oils that can burn your skin and eyes, avoid direct contact with chiles as much as possible. When working with chile peppers, wear plastic or rubber gloves. If your bare hands do touch chile peppers, wash your hands well with soap and water.

Nutrition Facts per serving: 272 cal., 17 g total fat (7 g sat. fat), 103 mg chol., 235 mg sodium, 1 g carbo., 0 g fiber, 28 g pro.
Daily Values: 5% vit. A, 3% vit. C, 2% calcium, 7% iron

2
net carbs

Hot Barbecued Chicken

Prep: 10 minutes Marinate: 2 hours Grill: 50 minutes Makes: 6 servings
  2½ to 3 pounds meaty chicken pieces (breast halves, thighs, and drumsticks)
   1 2-ounce bottle (¼ cup) hot pepper sauce
   3 tablespoons catsup
   3 tablespoons Worcestershire sauce

1 Place chicken pieces in a self-sealing plastic bag set in a shallow dish. For marinade, combine the hot pepper sauce, catsup, and Worcestershire sauce. Pour over chicken pieces; seal bag. Marinate in refrigerator for 2 to 3 hours.

2 Drain chicken, discarding marinade. For a charcoal grill, arrange medium-hot coals around a drip pan. Test for medium heat above the pan. Place chicken pieces, bone sides down, on a grill rack over drip pan. Cover and grill for 50 to 60 minutes or until chicken is no longer pink (170°F for breasts; 180°F for thighs and drumsticks). (For a gas grill, preheat grill. Reduce heat to medium. Adjust for indirect cooking. Grill as above.)

Nutrition Facts per serving: 285 cal., 17 g total fat (5 g sat. fat), 110 mg chol., 201 mg sodium, 2 g carbo., 0 g fiber, 29 g pro. Daily Values: 5% vit. A, 6% vit. C, 2% calcium, 8% iron

Tuscan Chicken

If you can't find pesto seasoning, substitute dried Italian seasoning.

Start to Finish: 50 minutes Makes: 4 servings

- 2 to 2½ pounds meaty chicken pieces (breast halves, thighs, and drumsticks)
- 2 tablespoons olive oil
- 1¼ teaspoons pesto seasoning
- ½ cup whole kalamata olives
- ½ cup white wine or chicken broth

1 In a 12-inch skillet cook the chicken pieces in hot oil over medium heat for 15 minutes, turning to brown evenly. Reduce heat. Drain off excess oil in skillet. Sprinkle pesto seasoning evenly over chicken. Add olives to skillet. Pour wine over all.

2 Simmer, covered, for 25 minutes. Uncover; cook for 5 to 10 minutes more or until chicken is no longer pink (170°F for breasts; 180°F for thighs and drumsticks).

Nutrition Facts per serving: 334 cal., 18 g total fat (4 g sat. fat), 104 mg chol., 280 mg sodium, 2 g carbo., 1 g fiber, 34 g pro. **Daily Values:** 1% vit. A, 3% calcium, 9% iron

6
net carbs

Pesto-Stuffed Chicken Breasts

Prep: 20 minutes Bake: 45 minutes Oven: 375°F Makes: 4 servings

- 4 chicken breast halves with skin and bone
- ½ cup roasted red sweet peppers, drained and chopped
- ⅓ cup purchased basil pesto
- 2 tablespoons finely shredded Parmesan cheese
  Salt and black pepper
- 1 tablespoon butter, melted

1 Using your fingers, gently separate the chicken skin from the meat of the breasts along rib edge.

2 For stuffing, in a small bowl combine sweet peppers, pesto, and Parmesan cheese. Spoon a rounded tablespoon of stuffing between the skin and meat of each breast. Sprinkle stuffed chicken breasts with salt and black pepper.

3 Place chicken pieces, bone sides down, in a greased 2-quart rectangular baking dish. Drizzle with melted butter. Bake, uncovered, in a 375° oven for 45 to 55 minutes or until chicken is no longer pink (170°F).

Nutrition Facts per serving: 422 cal., 23 g total fat (5 g sat. fat), 113 mg chol., 625 mg sodium, 6 g carbo., 0 g fiber, 45 g pro.
Daily Values: 5% vit. A, 88% vit. C, 23% calcium, 8% iron

Mustard Baked Chicken

Prep: 10 minutes Bake: 35 minutes Oven: 425°F Makes: 6 servings
- 2½ to 3 pounds meaty chicken pieces (breast halves, thighs, and drumsticks)
- ⅓ cup brown mustard
- 1 tablespoon cooking oil
- 1 tablespoon soy sauce
- 2 teaspoons no-calorie heat-stable granular sugar substitute (Splenda)

1 Skin chicken, if desired. Place chicken in a lightly greased shallow baking pan. Bake in a 425° oven for 15 minutes.

2 Meanwhile, in a small bowl stir together mustard, oil, soy sauce, and sugar substitute. Brush mustard mixture generously over chicken pieces. Bake for 20 to 25 minutes more or until chicken is no longer pink (170°F for breasts; 180°F for thighs and drumsticks), brushing frequently with mustard mixture.

Nutrition Facts per serving: 259 cal., 14 g total fat (3 g sat. fat), 86 mg chol., 409 mg sodium, 4 g carbo., 0 g fiber, 29 g pro. Daily Values: 3% calcium, 8% iron

Lemon Chicken with Garlic and Rosemary

This easy baked chicken features rosemary, lemon, and garlic, classic Mediterranean flavors. Asparagus makes a pleasing accompaniment.

Prep: 15 minutes Bake: 35 minutes Oven: 425°F Makes: 6 servings

- 1 tablespoon snipped fresh rosemary or 1 teaspoon dried rosemary, crushed
- 1 teaspoon salt
- 1 teaspoon coarsely ground black pepper
- 2½ to 3 pounds meaty chicken pieces (breast halves, thighs, and drumsticks)
- 1 medium lemon
- 2 tablespoons olive oil
- 2 cloves garlic, minced

1 In a small bowl combine rosemary, salt, and pepper. Using your fingers, rub rosemary mixture onto both sides of chicken pieces. Place chicken pieces, bone sides up, in a lightly greased 13×9×2-inch baking pan.

2 Finely shred 1 teaspoon peel from the lemon. Cut lemon in half; squeeze lemon until you have 1 tablespoon juice. In a small bowl combine lemon peel, lemon juice, oil, and garlic; drizzle over chicken.

3 Bake in a 425° oven for 20 minutes. Turn chicken pieces bone sides down; spoon pan juices over chicken pieces. Bake for 15 to 20 minutes more or until chicken is no longer pink (170°F for breasts; 180°F for thighs and drumsticks).

Nutrition Facts per serving: 257 cal., 15 g total fat (4 g sat. fat), 86 mg chol., 464 mg sodium, 1 g carbo., 0 g fiber, 28 g pro.
Daily Values: 3% vit. C, 2% calcium, 7% iron

Sesame Chicken

Prep: 15 minutes Bake: 45 minutes Oven: 400°F Makes: 4 servings

   Nonstick cooking spray
3   tablespoons sesame seeds
3   tablespoons unbleached flour
¼   teaspoon salt
¼   teaspoon black pepper
4   chicken breast halves with skin and bone
3   tablespoons reduced-sodium teriyaki sauce
1   tablespoon butter, melted

1 Lightly coat a shallow baking pan with cooking spray; set pan aside. In a large plastic bag combine sesame seeds, flour, salt, and pepper. If desired, remove skin from chicken. Dip chicken in teriyaki sauce. Add chicken to flour mixture in plastic bag, shaking bag to coat chicken.

2 Place chicken pieces, bone sides down, in prepared baking pan. Drizzle with melted butter. Bake, uncovered, in a 400° oven about 45 minutes or until chicken is no longer pink (170°F).

Nutrition Facts per serving: 393 cal., 21 g total fat (7 g sat. fat), 123 mg chol., 510 mg sodium, 8 g carbo., 1 g fiber, 40 g pro.
Daily Values: 5% vit. A, 2% vit. C, 3% calcium, 11% iron

1
net carbs

Wine-Marinated Grilled Chicken Breasts

An easy marinade that's seasoned with Italian herbs and garlic makes this chicken a must at your next backyard cookout.

Prep: 20 minutes   Marinate: 8 to 24 hours   Grill: 50 minutes   Makes: 4 to 6 servings

- 4 to 6 medium chicken breast halves (2 to 3 pounds total)
- 1½ cups dry white wine
- ½ cup olive oil
- 1 tablespoon dried Italian seasoning, crushed
- 4 cloves garlic, minced (2 teaspoons)

1 If desired, remove skin from the chicken breasts. Place chicken in a self-sealing plastic bag set in a shallow dish.

2 For marinade, in a small bowl stir together the wine, olive oil, Italian seasoning, and garlic. Pour over the chicken; seal bag. Marinate in the refrigerator for 8 to 24 hours, turning bag occasionally.

3 Drain chicken, reserving the marinade. For a charcoal grill, arrange medium-hot coals around a drip pan. Test for medium heat above the pan. Place chicken breasts, bone sides up, on grill rack over drip pan. Cover and grill for 50 to 60 minutes or until no longer pink (170°F), turning once and brushing the chicken with the reserved marinade halfway through grilling. (For a gas grill, preheat grill. Reduce heat to medium. Adjust for indirect cooking. Grill as above.) Discard the remaining marinade.

Nutrition Facts per serving: 402 cal., 24 g total fat (6 g sat. fat), 115 mg chol., 93 mg sodium, 1 g carbo., 0 g fiber, 38 g pro.
Daily Values: 2% vit. A, 3% vit. C, 3% calcium, 9% iron

Indian-Style Chicken

If you prefer flavorful dark meat, this recipe is for you. The robust four-ingredient sauce is just right with drumsticks and thighs.

Prep: 5 minutes Grill: 35 minutes Makes: 6 servings
- ½ cup bottled low-carb barbecue sauce
- ¼ cup natural peanut butter
- ½ teaspoon finely shredded orange peel
- 1 to 2 tablespoons orange juice
- 1½ pounds chicken drumsticks and/or thighs

1 For sauce, stir together barbecue sauce, peanut butter, orange peel, and enough orange juice to make desired consistency. Set sauce aside.

2 For a charcoal grill, grill chicken on the rack of an uncovered grill directly over medium coals for 35 to 45 minutes or until chicken is no longer pink (180°F), turning once and brushing with sauce during the last 5 minutes of grilling. (For a gas grill, preheat grill. Reduce heat to medium. Place chicken on grill rack over heat. Cover and grill as above.)

3 If desired, place any remaining sauce in a 1-cup glass measure. Microwave on 100% power (high) for 30 to 60 seconds or until boiling. Serve with chicken.

Nutrition Facts per serving: 201 cal., 13 g total fat (1 g sat. fat), 68 mg chol., 267 mg sodium, 5 g carbo., 1 g fiber, 15 g pro. Daily Values: 3% vit. C, 1% iron

0
net carbs

Garlicky Grilled Chicken

Prep: 15 minutes Grill: 1 hour Stand: 10 minutes Makes: 4 servings

 1 2½- to 3-pound whole roasting chicken
 1 tablespoon cooking oil
 2 cloves garlic, minced
    Salt and ground black pepper
 1 teaspoon dark roast ground coffee

1 Rinse inside of chicken; pat dry with paper towels. Skewer neck skin of chicken to back; tie legs to tail. Twist wing tips under back. In a small bowl stir together oil and garlic. Brush chicken with garlic mixture. Sprinkle with salt, pepper, and ground coffee. If desired, insert a meat thermometer into center of an inside thigh muscle, not touching bone.

2 For a charcoal grill, arrange medium-hot coals around a drip pan. Test for medium heat above the pan. Place chicken, breast side up, on grill rack over drip pan. Cover and grill for 1 to 1¼ hours or until drumsticks move easily in their sockets and chicken is no longer pink (180°F). (For a gas grill, preheat grill. Reduce heat to medium. Adjust for indirect cooking. Grill as above.)

3 Remove chicken from grill. Cover with foil and let stand for 10 minutes before serving.

Nutrition Facts per serving: 200 cal., 12 g total fat (3 g sat. fat), 66 mg chol., 110 mg sodium, 0 g carbo., 0 g fiber, 20 g pro.
Daily Values: 1% vit. C, 1% calcium, 5% iron

Fresh Garlic and Pecan Chicken
Roast chicken gets a crunchy twist with this butter and pecan coating.

Prep: 30 minutes Roast: 1¼ hours Stand: 10 minutes Oven: 375°F Makes: 4 servings

1 3- to 3½-pound whole broiler-fryer chicken
6 cloves garlic, thinly sliced
⅔ cup finely chopped pecans
¼ cup butter, melted
1 tablespoon snipped fresh thyme or 1 teaspoon dried thyme, crushed
½ teaspoon black pepper
¼ teaspoon salt

1 Rinse inside of chicken; pat dry with paper towels. Skewer neck skin of chicken to back; tie legs to tail. Twist wing tips under back. Using a small, sharp knife, make numerous slits about 1 inch wide and ½ inch deep in the breast portions of the chicken. Stuff garlic in slits.

2 In a small bowl combine pecans, melted butter, thyme, pepper, and salt. Pat mixture onto top of chicken.

3 Place chicken, breast side up, on a rack in a shallow roasting pan. If desired, insert a meat thermometer into center of an inside thigh muscle, not touching bone.

4 Roast, uncovered, in a 375° oven for 1¼ to 1½ hours or until drumsticks move easily in their sockets and chicken is no longer pink (180°F). (If necessary, cover chicken loosely with foil for the last 10 to 15 minutes of roasting to prevent pecans from overbrowning.) Remove chicken from oven. Cover and let stand for 10 minutes before serving. If desired, spoon any pecans from roasting pan over each serving.

Nutrition Facts per serving: 725 cal., 59 g total fat (18 g sat. fat), 205 mg chol., 400 mg sodium, 4 g carbo., 2 g fiber, 45 g pro.
Daily Values: 15% vit. A, 9% vit. C, 5% calcium, 15% iron

2
net carbs

Roasted Italian Chicken

Prep: 15 minutes Roast: 1¼ hours Stand: 10 minutes Oven: 375°F Makes: 6 servings

    2   tablespoons balsamic vinegar
    2   tablespoons olive oil
    1   tablespoon lemon juice
    3   cloves garlic, minced
    ½   teaspoon salt
    ½   teaspoon coarsely ground black pepper
    1   tablespoon snipped fresh oregano or 1 teaspoon dried oregano, crushed
    1   tablespoon snipped fresh basil or 1 teaspoon dried basil, crushed
  1½   teaspoons snipped fresh thyme or ½ teaspoon thyme, crushed
    1   3- to 3½-pound whole broiler-fryer chicken

1 In a small bowl whisk together vinegar, oil, lemon juice, garlic, salt, pepper, oregano, basil, and thyme. Set aside.

2 Rinse inside of chicken; pat dry with paper towels. Place chicken, breast side up, on a rack in a shallow roasting pan. Tie legs to tail. Twist wing tips under back. Slip your fingers between the skin and the breast and leg meat of the chicken, forming a pocket. Spoon herb mixture into pocket. If desired, insert a meat thermometer into center of an inside thigh muscle, not touching bone.

3 Roast, uncovered, in a 375° oven for 1¼ to 1½ hours or until drumsticks move easily in their sockets and chicken is no longer pink (180°F). Remove chicken from oven. Cover with foil; let stand for 10 minutes before carving.

Nutrition Facts per serving: 266 cal., 17 g total fat (4 g sat. fat), 79 mg chol., 268 mg sodium, 2 g carbo., 0 g fiber, 25 g pro. Daily Values: 5% vit. A, 2% vit. C, 3% calcium, 8% iron

Hoisin-Sauced Cornish Hens

Prep: 15 minutes Roast: 1¼ hours Oven: 375°F Makes: 4 servings

- 2 1¼- to 1½-pound Cornish game hens, halved lengthwise
  Salt
- ½ cup bottled hoisin sauce
- ¼ cup raspberry or red wine vinegar
- ¼ cup orange juice
- 1 to 2 teaspoons red chile paste

1 Sprinkle hens with salt. Place hens, breast sides up, on a rack in a shallow roasting pan. Cover loosely with foil. Roast in a 375° oven for 30 minutes.

2 Meanwhile, in a small bowl stir together hoisin sauce, vinegar, orange juice, and red chile paste. Brush some of the hoisin sauce mixture over hens. Roast, uncovered, for 45 to 60 minutes more or until an instant-read thermometer inserted into the thighs of each hen registers 180°F, brushing occasionally with remaining hoisin sauce mixture.

Nutrition Facts per serving: 371 cal., 23 g total fat (5 g sat. fat), 120 mg chol., 2,223 mg sodium, 6 g carbo., 0 g fiber, 38 g pro. Daily Values: 13% vit. C, 5% iron

2 net carbs

Turkey with Onion-Cilantro Relish

Prep: 5 minutes Grill: 15 minutes Makes: 4 servings
- ½ cup chopped onion
- ¼ cup fresh cilantro sprigs
- ⅛ teaspoon salt
- ⅛ teaspoon black pepper
- 2 turkey breast tenderloins, halved horizontally (about 1 pound total)
- 3 tablespoons lime or lemon juice

1 In a blender or food processor combine onion, cilantro, salt, and pepper; cover and blend or process until mixture is very finely chopped.

2 Dip turkey in lime juice. For a charcoal grill, grill turkey on the rack of an uncovered grill directly over medium coals for 7 minutes. Turn and brush with lime juice. Spread the onion mixture over turkey. Grill for 8 to 11 minutes more or until turkey is no longer pink (170°F). (For a gas grill, preheat grill. Reduce heat to medium. Place turkey on grill rack over heat. Cover and grill as above.)

Nutrition Facts per serving: 141 cal., 2 g total fat (1 g sat. fat), 68 mg chol., 130 mg sodium, 3 g carbo., 1 g fiber, 27 g pro.
Daily Values: 6% vit. A, 10% vit. C, 3% calcium, 8% iron

Parmesan-Sesame-Crusted Turkey

Prep: 15 minutes Cook: 8 minutes Makes: 4 servings
- ½ cup finely shredded Parmesan cheese
- ¼ cup sesame seeds
- 1 beaten egg
- 4 turkey breast slices, ½ inch thick
- ¼ teaspoon salt
- ¼ teaspoon black pepper
- 1 tablespoon olive oil or cooking oil

1 In a shallow dish or pie plate combine Parmesan cheese and sesame seeds. Place egg in another shallow dish or pie plate. Dip turkey slices into egg; coat with Parmesan cheese mixture. Sprinkle each turkey slice with salt and pepper.

2 In a large skillet cook turkey in hot oil over medium-high heat for 8 to 10 minutes or until turkey is no longer pink (170°F), turning once.

Nutrition Facts per serving: 498 cal., 28 g total fat (13 g sat. fat), 171 mg chol., 1,336 mg sodium, 3 g carbo., 1 g fiber, 57 g pro. Daily Values: 10% vit. A, 87% calcium, 15% iron

2
net carbs

Bacon-Wrapped Turkey Mignons

To partially cook bacon, arrange the slices in a large skillet and cook over medium heat until lightly browned but still limp, turning once. Drain the bacon on paper towels and cool until easy to handle.

Prep: 25 minutes   Bake: 30 minutes   Oven: 400°F   Makes: 6 servings

- 2 turkey breast steaks
    Salt and black pepper
- 6 slices bacon, partially cooked and drained
- ¼ cup bottled honey-mustard dipping sauce

1 Season turkey with salt and pepper. Cut both turkey steaks crosswise into 4 pieces. Press the two end pieces of each turkey steak together to form one piece (you should have six "mignons"). Wrap 1 slice of bacon around each piece of turkey; secure with wooden toothpicks.

2 Place turkey in a 13×9×2-inch baking pan. Bake in a 400° oven for 30 to 40 minutes or until turkey is no longer pink (170°F), brushing with dipping sauce the last 15 minutes of baking.

Nutrition Facts per serving: 239 cal., 7 g total fat (2 g sat. fat), 109 mg chol., 401 mg sodium, 2 g carbo., 0 g fiber, 39 g pro.
Daily Values: 2% calcium, 11% iron

Turkey Tenderloins with Cilantro Pesto

Place a small amount of the pesto in a separate small bowl and use that to brush over the chicken during grilling. Chill the remaining pesto in the refrigerator until serving.

Prep: 15 minutes Grill: 12 minutes Makes: 8 servings
- 1½ cups lightly packed fresh cilantro sprigs or fresh basil leaves
- ⅓ cup walnuts
- 3 tablespoons olive oil
- 3 tablespoons lime juice
- 2 cloves garlic, minced
- ¼ teaspoon salt
- 4 turkey breast tenderloins, halved horizontally (2 pounds)
  Lime or lemon wedges (optional)

1 For pesto, in a blender or food processor place cilantro, walnuts, olive oil, lime juice, garlic, and salt. Cover and blend or process until nearly smooth. Cover and store in the refrigerator for 1 to 2 days.

2 Season turkey with salt and pepper. For a charcoal grill, grill turkey on the rack of an uncovered grill directly over medium coals 7 minutes. Brush lightly with cilantro pesto. Grill for 5 to 8 minutes more or until turkey is no longer pink (170°F). (For a gas grill, preheat grill. Reduce heat to medium. Place turkey on grill rack over heat. Cover and grill as above.)

3 Serve with remaining pesto. If desired, serve with lime wedges to squeeze over tenderloins.

Nutrition Facts per serving: 213 cal., 10 g total fat (2 g sat. fat), 68 mg chol., 134 mg sodium, 2 g carbo., 1 g fiber, 28 g pro.
Daily Values: 18% vit. A, 12% vit. C, 3% calcium, 9% iron

Grilled Turkey Piccata

If you can't find turkey tenderloin steaks at your supermarket, buy whole turkey tenderloins and cut them horizontally into ½-inch slices.

Prep: 15 minutes Grill: 12 minutes Makes: 4 servings

- 2 lemons
- 4 teaspoons olive oil
- 2 teaspoons snipped fresh rosemary or ½ teaspoon dried rosemary, crushed
- ¼ teaspoon salt
- ¼ teaspoon freshly ground black pepper
- 4 ½-inch-thick turkey breast tenderloin steaks (about 1¼ to 1½ pounds)
- 1 tablespoon drained capers
- 1 tablespoon snipped fresh flat-leaf parsley

1 Finely shred enough peel from 1 of the lemons to make 1 teaspoon; set shredded peel aside. Halve and squeeze the juice from the lemon (should have about 3 tablespoons); set juice aside. Cut remaining lemon into very thin slices; set aside.

2 For rub, in a small bowl combine the shredded lemon peel, 2 teaspoons of the olive oil, the rosemary, salt, and pepper. Sprinkle the mixture evenly over both sides of turkey steaks; rub in with your fingers.

3 For a charcoal grill, grill turkey on the rack of an uncovered grill directly over medium coals for 6 minutes. Arrange lemon slices on top of turkey, overlapping if necessary. Cover and grill for 6 to 9 minutes more or until turkey is no longer pink (170°F). (For a gas grill, preheat gas grill. Reduce heat to medium. Place turkey on the grill rack over heat. Cover and grill as above.)

4 Meanwhile, in a small saucepan combine the remaining olive oil, the lemon juice, and the capers. Heat through. Remove turkey steaks to a serving platter. Drizzle turkey with the warm caper mixture. Sprinkle with snipped parsley.

Nutrition Facts per serving: 159 cal., 5 g total fat (1 g sat. fat), 71 mg chol., 269 mg sodium, 1 g carbo., 0 g fiber, 26 g pro.
Daily Values: 1% vit. A, 12% vit. C, 1% calcium, 8% iron

chapter 3

Fish and Seafood

3
net carbs

Fish Fillets with Yogurt Dressing

When marinating fish and shellfish, do not exceed the maximum marinating time. Otherwise it will be tough and chewy when cooked.

Prep: 15 minutes Marinate: 20 to 30 minutes Bake: 4 to 6 minutes per ½-inch thickness
Oven: 450°F Makes: 4 servings

- 1 pound fresh or frozen skinless cod, orange roughy, or other fish fillets, ½ to 1 inch thick
- ⅔ cup bottled poppy seed salad dressing
- 3 tablespoons thinly sliced green onions
- 1 teaspoon snipped fresh thyme
- ½ cup plain yogurt

1 Thaw fish, if frozen. Rinse fish; pat dry with paper towels. If necessary, cut fish into 4 serving-size pieces. For marinade, in a shallow dish combine ½ cup of the salad dressing, 2 tablespoons of the green onions, and ½ teaspoon of the thyme. Add fish; turn to coat with marinade. Cover and marinate in refrigerator for 20 to 30 minutes. Drain fish, discarding the marinade.

2 Measure thickness of fish. Arrange fish in a greased 2-quart rectangular baking dish. Tuck under any thin edges. Bake in a 450° oven until fish flakes easily when tested with a fork (allow 4 to 6 minutes per ½-inch thickness of fish).

3 Meanwhile, for sauce, combine yogurt, the remaining salad dressing, remaining 1 tablespoon green onions, and remaining ½ teaspoon thyme. Serve sauce with fish.

Nutrition Facts per serving: 182 cal., 9 g total fat (2 g sat. fat), 55 mg chol., 201 mg sodium, 3 g carbo., 0 g fiber, 22 g pro.
Daily Values: 2% vit. A, 3% vit. C, 7% calcium, 3% iron

Parmesan Baked Salmon

Prep: 15 minutes Bake: 4 to 6 minutes per ½-inch thickness
Oven: 450°F Makes: 4 servings

- 4 4-ounce fresh or frozen skinless salmon fillets or other fish fillets, ¾ to 1 inch thick
  Nonstick cooking spray
- ¼ cup mayonnaise
- 2 tablespoons grated Parmesan cheese
- 1 tablespoon snipped fresh chives or sliced green onion
- 1 teaspoon white wine Worcestershire sauce

1 Thaw fish, if frozen. Rinse fish; pat dry with paper towels. Lightly coat a 2-quart rectangular baking dish with cooking spray. Arrange fish in prepared dish. Tuck under any thin edges.

2 In a small bowl stir together mayonnaise, Parmesan cheese, chives, and Worcestershire sauce; spread over fish. Bake in a 450° oven until fish flakes easily when tested with a fork (allow 4 to 6 minutes per ½-inch thickness of fish).

Nutrition Facts per serving: 252 cal., 16 g total fat (3 g sat. fat), 77 mg chol., 200 mg sodium, 2 g carbo., 0 g fiber, 25 g pro.
Daily Values: 5% vit. A, 1% vit. C, 4% calcium, 3% iron

Cajun Catfish with Coleslaw

Salt-free Cajun seasoning has a zippier flavor and richer color than the regular Cajun seasonings, most of which contain salt. If you use regular Cajun seasoning, omit the salt.

Prep: 10 minutes Bake: 15 minutes Oven: 350°F Makes: 4 servings

- 1 pound fresh or frozen skinless catfish fillets, ½ inch thick
- 2½ teaspoons salt-free Cajun seasoning
- ¼ teaspoon salt
- 2 cups shredded cabbage with carrot (coleslaw mix)
- 3 tablespoons mayonnaise
  Salt and black pepper (optional)
  Bottled hot pepper sauce (optional)

1 Thaw fish, if frozen. Rinse fish; pat dry with paper towels. If necessary, cut fish into 4 serving-size pieces.

2 Combine 2 teaspoons of the Cajun seasoning and the ¼ teaspoon salt; sprinkle both sides of fish with seasoning mixture. Arrange fish in a greased 3-quart rectangular baking dish. Tuck under any thin edges. Bake in a 350° oven for 15 to 20 minutes or until fish flakes easily when tested with a fork.

3 Meanwhile, in a medium bowl stir together cabbage, mayonnaise, and the remaining ½ teaspoon Cajun seasoning. If desired, season to taste with salt and pepper. Cover and chill until serving time. Serve catfish with coleslaw and, if desired, hot pepper sauce.

Nutrition Facts per serving: 241 cal., 17 g total fat (3 g sat. fat), 57 mg chol., 127 mg sodium, 3 g carbo., 1 g fiber, 18 g pro.
Daily Values: 2% vit. A, 20% vit. C, 4% calcium, 6% iron

South-of-the-Border Snapper

net carbs

Prep: 5 minutes Bake: 15 minutes Oven: 425°F Makes: 4 servings
- 4 4-ounce fresh or frozen red snapper, orange roughy, sole, or cod fillets, ½ inch thick
- ½ cup bottled chunky salsa
- ¾ cup shredded Monterey Jack and/or cheddar cheese

1 Thaw fish, if frozen. Rinse fish; pat dry with paper towels. Arrange fish in a 2-quart rectangular baking dish. Tuck under any thin edges. Spoon salsa over fish; sprinkle with cheese. Bake in a 425° oven about 15 minutes or until fish flakes easily when tested with a fork.

Nutrition Facts per serving: 195 cal., 8 g total fat (4 g sat. fat), 60 mg chol., 255 mg sodium, 1 g carbo., 0 g fiber, 29 g pro.
Daily Values: 8% vit. A, 6% vit. C, 20% calcium, 3% iron

3

net carbs

Flounder Bundles

Bundle fish, shallots, and lemon juice in foil packets for easy entrées. Serve the fish right from the package it was cooked in.

Prep: 15 minutes Bake: 15 minutes Oven: 400°F Makes: 4 servings

- 4 4-ounce fresh or frozen flounder or sole fillets, ½ inch thick
- 2 tablespoons lemon juice
- 2 tablespoons finely chopped shallots
- 1 clove garlic, minced
- ⅛ teaspoon black pepper
- ¼ cup purchased basil pesto

1 Thaw fish, if frozen. Rinse fish; pat dry with paper towels. Place each fillet on a 9×9-inch piece of heavy foil. Fold each fillet crosswise in half.

2 In a small bowl stir together lemon juice, shallots, garlic, and pepper; spoon over fish. Top with pesto. Bring together 2 opposite edges of foil and seal with a double fold. Fold remaining ends to completely enclose food, allowing space for steam to build. Place foil packets in a 15×10×1-inch baking pan.

3 Bake in a 400° oven about 15 minutes or until fish flakes easily when tested with a fork. Open carefully to allow steam to escape. Transfer packets to serving plates.

Nutrition Facts per serving: 173 cal., 9 g total fat (1 g sat. fat), 54 mg chol., 199 mg sodium, 3 g carbo., 0 g fiber, 21 g pro.
Daily Values: 4% vit. A, 7% vit. C, 6% calcium, 7% iron

Vegetable-Topped Fish

4 net carbs

Start to Finish: 15 minutes Oven: 450°F Makes: 4 servings
- 1 pound fresh or frozen fish fillets
- 2 teaspoons butter, melted
- ⅛ teaspoon salt
- ⅛ teaspoon black pepper
- 1 cup bottled salsa
- 1 small yellow summer squash or zucchini, halved lengthwise and cut into ¼-inch slices

1 Thaw fish, if frozen. Rinse fish; pat dry with paper towels. Cut fish into 4 serving-size pieces, if necessary. Measure thickness of fish. Place fish on a greased baking sheet. Tuck under any thin edges. Brush fish with melted butter; sprinkle with salt and pepper. Bake in a 450° oven until fish flakes easily when tested with a fork (allow 4 to 6 minutes per ½-inch thickness of fish).

2 Meanwhile, in a small saucepan stir together salsa and summer squash. Bring to boiling; reduce heat. Simmer, covered, for 5 to 6 minutes or until squash is crisp-tender. Serve over fish.

Nutrition Facts per serving: 131 cal., 3 g total fat (0 g sat. fat), 48 mg chol., 403 mg sodium, 5 g carbo., 1 g fiber, 22 g pro.
Daily Values: 10% vit. A, 21% vit. C, 4% calcium, 6% iron

3

net carbs

Salmon with Pesto Mayo

When toasting the crumbled bread under the broiler, watch carefully so the crumbs don't burn. Low-carb breads tend to burn more easily than regular breads.

Start to Finish: 20 minutes Makes: 4 servings

- 4   5- to 6-ounce fresh or frozen skinless salmon fillets
- 2   tablespoons crumbled low-carb bread
- ¼   cup mayonnaise
- 3   tablespoons purchased basil pesto
- 1   tablespoon grated Parmesan cheese

1 Thaw fish, if frozen. Rinse fish; pat dry with paper towels. Set fish aside. Preheat broiler. Place crumbled bread in a shallow baking pan. Broil 4 inches from heat for 1 to 2 minutes or until lightly toasted, stirring once. Set bread crumbs aside.

2 Measure thickness of fish. Place fish on the greased unheated rack of a broiler pan. Tuck under any thin edges. Broil 4 inches from the heat until fish flakes easily when tested with a fork (allow 4 to 6 minutes per ½-inch thickness of fish). (If fillets are 1 inch thick, turn once halfway through broiling.)

3 Meanwhile, in a small bowl stir together mayonnaise and pesto; set aside. Combine toasted bread crumbs and Parmesan cheese. Spoon mayonnaise mixture over fish; sprinkle with crumb mixture. Broil 1 to 2 minutes more or until crumbs are light brown.

Nutrition Facts per serving: 354 cal., 24 g total fat (3 g sat. fat), 81 mg chol., 283 mg sodium, 3 g carbo., 0 g fiber, 30 g pro. **Daily Values:** 4% vit. A, 4% calcium, 7% iron

Fish Tacos

A new and different taco! Save carbs by wrapping these spiced fish pieces in romaine lettuce leaves rather than tortillas. Top each serving with cooling lime sour cream.

Prep: 5 minutes Broil: 4 to 6 minutes per ½-inch thickness Makes: 4 servings
- 1 pound fresh or frozen skinless cod, orange roughy, or other fish fillets, ½ to ¾ inch thick
- 2 teaspoons Mexican seasoning blend
- ¼ teaspoon salt
- 1 medium lime
- ½ cup dairy sour cream
- 8 romaine lettuce leaves or four 8-inch low-carb tortillas

1 Thaw fish, if frozen. Rinse fish; pat dry with paper towels. Combine Mexican seasoning and salt; sprinkle both sides of fish with seasoning mixture. Preheat broiler. Place fish on the greased unheated rack of a broiler pan. Tuck under any thin edges. Broil 4 inches from heat until fish flakes easily when tested with a fork (allow 4 to 6 minutes per ½-inch thickness of fish).

2 Meanwhile, finely shred ½ teaspoon peel from lime. Cut lime in half; squeeze until you have 1 tablespoon juice. In a small bowl stir together lime peel, lime juice, and sour cream. Set aside.

3 Using a fork, flake fish into bite-size pieces. Serve fish pieces in romaine leaves with sour cream mixture.

Nutrition Facts per serving (with romaine): 154 cal., 6 g total fat (3 g sat. fat), 59 mg chol., 315 mg sodium, 3 g carbo., 0 g fiber, 22 g pro. Daily Values: 7% vit. A, 7% vit. C, 6% calcium, 5% iron

3 net carbs

Browned Butter Salmon

Prep: 20 minutes Broil: 8 minutes Makes: 4 servings

- 4 fresh or frozen salmon or halibut steaks, 1 inch thick
  Salt and black pepper
- 2 tablespoons butter
- 2 tablespoons reduced-calorie maple-flavor syrup
- 1 teaspoon finely shredded orange peel

1 Thaw fish, if frozen. Rinse fish; pat dry with paper towels. Sprinkle fish with salt and pepper; set fish aside.

2 In a small saucepan cook butter over medium heat about 3 minutes or until golden brown, stirring occasionally. Remove saucepan from heat; cool for 10 minutes. Stir in maple syrup and orange peel (mixture may thicken).

3 Preheat broiler. Place fish on the greased unheated rack of a foil-lined broiler pan. Spread both sides of fish with the browned butter mixture. Broil 4 inches from heat for 8 to 12 minutes or until fish flakes easily when tested with a fork, turning once halfway through broiling.

Nutrition Facts per serving: 264 cal., 12 g total fat (5 g sat. fat), 105 mg chol., 336 mg sodium, 3 g carbo., 0 g fiber, 34 g pro.
Daily Values: 8% vit. A, 1% vit. C, 3% calcium, 7% iron

Fish Fillets with Salsa Verde

Snipped cilantro freshens the taste of bottled green salsa.

Prep: 10 minutes Broil: 4 to 6 minutes per ½-inch thickness Makes: 4 servings
- 1 pound fresh or frozen cod or orange roughy fillets
- 1 medium lime
- 1 tablespoon olive oil
- ⅛ teaspoon salt
- ⅛ teaspoon black pepper
- ½ cup bottled green salsa
- 3 tablespoons snipped fresh cilantro

1 Thaw fish, if frozen. Rinse fish; pat dry with paper towels. Cut lime in half; squeeze one half until you have 1 tablespoon juice. Cut remaining lime half into wedges; set wedges aside. In a small bowl combine lime juice, oil, salt, and pepper. Brush fish with lime juice mixture.

2 Preheat broiler. Measure thickness of fish. Place the fish on the greased unheated rack of a broiler pan. Tuck under any thin edges. Broil 4 inches from heat until fish flakes easily when tested with a fork (allow 4 to 6 minutes per ½-inch thickness of fish). (If fillets are 1 inch thick, turn once halfway through broiling.)

3 Meanwhile, in a small bowl stir together green salsa and 2 tablespoons of the cilantro. Top fish with salsa mixture; sprinkle with the remaining 1 tablespoon cilantro. Serve with lime wedges.

Nutrition Facts per serving: 125 cal., 4 g total fat (1 g sat. fat), 42 mg chol., 157 mg sodium, 1 g carbo., 0 g fiber, 20 g pro.
Daily Values: 5% vit. A, 9% vit. C, 1% calcium, 2% iron

2 net carbs

Broiled Snapper with Fennel

Prep: 15 minutes Broil: 4 to 6 minutes per ½-inch thickness Makes: 4 servings

- 4 6- to 8-ounce fresh or frozen red snapper fillets
     Salt and black pepper
- 1 medium lemon
- 1 fennel bulb, trimmed and cut crosswise into thin slices (about 1¼ cups)
- 1 tablespoon butter
- 1 teaspoon snipped fresh dill or thyme

1 Thaw fish, if frozen. Rinse fish; pat dry with paper towels. Preheat broiler. Measure thickness of fish. Place fish on the greased unheated rack of a broiler pan. Sprinkle fish with salt and pepper. Broil 4 inches from heat until fish flakes easily when tested with a fork (allow 4 to 6 minutes per ½-inch thickness of fish).

2 Meanwhile, finely shred 1 teaspoon peel from lemon. Cut lemon in half; squeeze one half until you have 4 teaspoons juice. Cut remaining lemon half into wedges; set wedges aside.

3 In a small saucepan cook fennel in hot butter for 5 to 8 minutes or just until tender. Stir in lemon peel, lemon juice, and dill. Season to taste with salt and pepper. Spoon fennel over fish. Serve with lemon wedges.

Nutrition Facts per serving: 237 cal., 6 g total fat (2 g sat. fat), 81 mg chol., 318 mg sodium, 4 g carbo., 2 g fiber, 41 g pro.
Daily Values: 7% vit. A, 32% vit. C, 9% calcium, 4% iron

Orange Roughy with Lemon Butter

Prep: 10 minutes Broil: 4 to 6 minutes per ½-inch thickness Makes: 6 servings

- 1½ pounds fresh or frozen orange roughy, cod, or haddock fillets
- 2 tablespoons butter, melted
- 1 to 2 tablespoons lemon juice
  Salt and black pepper
  Snipped fresh parsley

1 Thaw fish, if frozen. Rinse fish; pat dry with paper towels. Preheat broiler. Measure thickness of fish. Place fish on the greased rack of an unheated broiler pan. Tuck under any thin edges. Combine melted butter and lemon juice; brush over fish. Sprinkle fish with salt and pepper.

2 Broil 4 inches from heat until fish flakes easily when tested with a fork, brushing occasionally with butter mixture (allow 4 to 6 minutes per ½-inch thickness of fish). Sprinkle with parsley.

Nutrition Facts per serving: 115 cal., 5 g total fat (3 g sat. fat), 33 mg chol., 210 mg sodium, 0 g carbo., 0 g fiber, 17 g pro.
Daily Values: 5% vit. A, 3% vit. C, 4% calcium, 1% iron

net carbs

Halibut with Tomatoes and Olives

Prep: 15 minutes Broil: 8 minutes Makes: 4 servings
- 4   6-ounce fresh or frozen halibut steaks, 1 inch thick
- 2   tablespoons olive oil
-     Salt and black pepper
- ⅓   cup chopped tomato
- ⅓   cup Greek black olives, pitted and chopped
- 2   tablespoons snipped fresh flat-leaf parsley or 1 tablespoon snipped fresh oregano or thyme

1 Thaw fish, if frozen. Rinse fish; pat dry with paper towels. Brush fish with 1 tablespoon of the oil; sprinkle with salt and pepper.

2 Preheat broiler. Place fish on the greased unheated rack of a broiler pan. Broil fish 4 inches from heat 8 to 12 minutes or until fish flakes easily when tested with a fork, turning once halfway through broiling.

3 Meanwhile, in a small bowl stir together the remaining 1 tablespoon oil, tomato, olives, and parsley. Spoon tomato mixture over fish.

Nutrition Facts per serving: 262 cal., 12 g total fat (2 g sat. fat), 54 mg chol., 264 mg sodium, 2 g carbo., 1 g fiber, 36 g pro.
Daily Values: 9% vit. A, 9% vit. C, 9% calcium, 11% iron

Sea Bass with Lemon-Caper Butter

If it's more convenient, make the lemon-caper butter ahead and store it in the refrigerator. Let stand at room temperature until softened before serving.

Prep: 10 minutes Broil: 8 minutes Makes: 4 servings

- 4 6-ounce fresh or frozen sea bass steaks, 1 inch thick
  Salt and black pepper
- 1 medium lemon
- ¼ cup butter, softened
- 1 tablespoon capers, drained
- 1 clove garlic, minced

1 Thaw fish, if frozen. Rinse fish; pat dry with paper towels. Preheat broiler. Sprinkle fish with salt and pepper. Place fish on the greased unheated rack of a broiler pan. Broil 4 inches from heat for 8 to 12 minutes or until fish flakes easily when tested with a fork, turning once halfway through broiling.

2 Meanwhile, finely shred 1 teaspoon peel from lemon. Cut lemon in half; squeeze one half until you have 2 teaspoons juice. Cut remaining lemon half into wedges; set wedges aside.

3 For lemon-caper butter, in a small bowl stir together lemon peel, lemon juice, butter, capers, and garlic. Top fish with butter mixture. Serve with lemon wedges.

Nutrition Facts per serving: 277 cal., 16 g total fat (8 g sat. fat), 102 mg chol., 449 mg sodium, 2 g carbo., 1 g fiber, 32 g pro. **Daily Values:** 15% vit. A, 21% vit. C, 3% calcium, 4% iron

Dilly Salmon Fillets

Prep: 15 minutes Marinate: 10 minutes Grill: 5 minutes Makes: 4 servings

4 6-ounce fresh or frozen skinless salmon fillets, ½ to ¾ inch thick
3 tablespoons lemon juice
2 tablespoons snipped fresh dill
2 tablespoons mayonnaise
2 teaspoons Dijon-style mustard

1 Thaw fish, if frozen. Rinse fish; pat dry with paper towels. For marinade, in a shallow dish combine lemon juice and 1 tablespoon of the dill. Add fish; turn to coat with marinade. Marinate at room temperature for 10 minutes. Meanwhile, in a small bowl stir together the remaining 1 tablespoon dill, the mayonnaise, and mustard; set aside.

2 For a charcoal grill, arrange medium-hot coals around a drip pan. Test for medium heat above pan. Place fish on greased grill rack over drip pan. Cover and grill for 3 minutes. Turn fish; spread with mayonnaise mixture. Cover and grill 2 to 6 minutes more or until fish flakes easily when tested with a fork. (For a gas grill, preheat grill. Reduce heat to medium. Adjust for indirect cooking. Grill as above.)

Nutrition Facts per serving: 211 cal., 11 g total fat (2 g sat. fat), 35 mg chol., 204 mg sodium, 1 g carbo., 0 g fiber, 25 g pro.
Daily Values: 4% vit. A, 8% vit. C, 1% calcium, 7% iron

Grilled Salmon with Tapenade

You can make the tapenade up to 24 hours before serving. Store it in a covered container in the refrigerator. Before serving, bring the tapenade to room temperature.

2
net carbs

Prep: 20 minutes Chill: 30 minutes Grill: 14 minutes Makes: 4 servings
- 1 1½-pound fresh or frozen skinless salmon fillet, 1 inch thick
- 2 tablespoons Dijon-style mustard
- ¼ teaspoon coarsely ground black pepper
- 1 recipe Tapenade or purchased bottled tapenade

1 Thaw fish, if frozen. Rinse fish; pat dry with paper towels. Cut fillet into 4 serving-size pieces. In a small bowl stir together mustard and pepper. Brush salmon on all sides with mustard mixture. Cover and chill for 30 minutes.

2 For a charcoal grill, arrange medium-hot coals around a drip pan. Test for medium heat above the pan. Place fish on a greased grill rack over the drip pan. Cover and grill for 14 to 18 minutes or until fish flakes easily when tested with a fork. (For a gas grill, preheat grill. Reduce heat to medium. Adjust for indirect cooking. Grill as above.) To serve, top each piece with Tapenade.

Tapenade: In a food processor combine ¼ cup oil-cured Greek olives, drained and pitted, or pitted ripe olives; ¼ cup pimiento-stuffed green olives; 1 clove garlic, minced; and 1 tablespoon olive oil (or oil from cured olives plus enough olive oil to equal 1 tablespoon). Cover and process until finely chopped. Add 2 tablespoons dried tomato pieces (not oil-packed). Cover and pulse twice or just until combined.

Nutrition Facts per serving: 336 cal., 19 g total fat (4 g sat. fat), 86 mg chol., 434 mg sodium, 3 g carbo., 1 g fiber, 37 g pro. Daily Values: 7% vit. A, 4% vit. C, 5% calcium, 8% iron

net carbs

Cilantro-Lime Orange Roughy

Prep: 10 minutes Grill: 4 to 6 minutes per ½-inch thickness Makes: 4 servings
- 1¼ pounds fresh or frozen orange roughy fillets, ¾ to 1 inch thick
  Salt and black pepper
- ¼ cup snipped fresh cilantro
- 1 tablespoon butter, melted
- 1 teaspoon finely shredded lime peel
- 1 tablespoon lime juice

1 Thaw fish, if frozen. Rinse fish; pat dry with paper towels. Cut fish into 4 serving-size pieces. Sprinkle with salt and pepper.

2 Place fish in a well-greased grill basket. Tuck under any thin edges. For a charcoal grill, grill fish on the rack of an uncovered grill directly over medium coals until fish flakes easily when tested with a fork, turning basket once (allow 4 to 6 minutes per ½-inch thickness of fish). (For a gas grill, preheat grill. Reduce heat to medium. Place fish on grill rack over heat. Cover and grill as above.)

3 Meanwhile, in a small bowl stir together cilantro, melted butter, lime peel, and lime juice. Spoon cilantro mixture over fish.

Nutrition Facts per serving: 127 cal., 4 g total fat (2 g sat. fat), 36 mg chol., 196 mg sodium, 1 g carbo., 0 g fiber, 21 g pro. Daily Values: 10% vit. A, 6% vit. C, 5% calcium, 2% iron

Mustard-Glazed Halibut Steaks

Although basil is the herb suggested for this easy fish entrée, other herbs, such as oregano or tarragon, are scrumptious choices too.

Prep: 10 minutes Grill: 8 minutes Makes: 4 servings
- 4 6-ounce fresh or frozen halibut steaks, cut 1 inch thick
- 2 tablespoons butter
- 2 tablespoons lemon juice
- 1 tablespoon Dijon-style mustard
- 2 teaspoons snipped fresh basil or ½ teaspoon dried basil, crushed

1 Thaw fish, if frozen. Rinse fish; pat dry with paper towels. In a small saucepan heat butter, lemon juice, mustard, and basil over low heat until butter is melted. Brush both sides of steaks with mustard mixture.

2 For a charcoal grill, grill fish on the greased rack of an uncovered grill directly over medium coals for 8 to 12 minutes or until fish flakes easily when tested with a fork, gently turning once halfway through grilling and brushing occasionally with mustard mixture. (For a gas grill, preheat grill. Reduce heat to medium. Place fish on greased grill rack over heat. Cover and grill as above.)

Nutrition Facts per serving: 243 cal., 10 g total fat (2 g sat. fat), 55 mg chol., 254 mg sodium, 1 g carbo., 0 g fiber, 36 g pro.
Daily Values: 5% vit. C, 6% calcium, 9% iron

2
net carbs

Swordfish with Cucumber Sauce

A refreshing sauce of yogurt, cucumber, and snipped mint tops these grilled fish steaks.

Prep: 10 minutes Grill: 8 minutes Makes: 4 servings
- 1 pound fresh or frozen swordfish or halibut steaks, ¾ inch thick
- ⅓ cup plain yogurt
- ¼ cup finely chopped cucumber
- 1 teaspoon snipped fresh mint or dill or ¼ teaspoon dried mint, crushed, or dried dill

1 Thaw fish, if frozen. Rinse fish; pat dry with paper towels. Cut into 4 serving-size pieces. For sauce, in a small bowl stir together yogurt, cucumber, and mint. Cover and chill until serving time.

2 For a charcoal grill, grill fish on the greased rack of an uncovered grill directly over medium coals for 8 to 12 minutes or until fish flakes easily when tested with a fork. (For a gas grill, preheat grill. Reduce heat to medium. Place fish on greased grill rack over heat. Cover and grill as above.) Serve with sauce.

Nutrition Facts per serving: 149 cal., 5 g total fat (1 g sat. fat), 44 mg chol., 116 mg sodium, 2 g carbo., 0 g fiber, 24 g pro.
Daily Values: 3% vit. A, 3% vit. C, 4% calcium, 6% iron

Grilled Trout

A grill basket puts the fun back into grilling small fish such as trout. Since you put all four fish into one basket, you can turn all of the fish at once and avoid the fish sticking to the grill rack.

Prep: 10 minutes Grill: 6 to 9 minutes Makes: 4 servings
- 4   8- to 10-ounce fresh or frozen dressed, boned rainbow trout
- 3   tablespoons lime juice
- 2   tablespoons olive oil
- 2   tablespoons snipped fresh cilantro or parsley
- ½   teaspoon kosher salt
- ¼   teaspoon freshly ground black pepper
- Lime wedges

1 Thaw fish, if frozen. Rinse fish; pat dry with paper towels. In a small bowl combine lime juice and olive oil; brush inside and outside of each fish with lime juice mixture. Combine cilantro, salt, and pepper; sprinkle insides of each fish cavity with cilantro mixture.

2 Place fish in a well-greased grill basket. For a charcoal grill, grill trout on the rack of an uncovered grill directly over medium coals for 6 to 9 minutes or until fish flakes easily when tested with a fork, turning basket once halfway through grilling. (For a gas grill, preheat grill. Reduce heat to medium. Place fish on grill rack over heat. Cover and grill as above.) Serve trout with lime wedges.

Nutrition Facts per serving: 376 cal., 19 g total fat (4 g sat. fat), 133 mg chol., 372 mg sodium, 1 g carbo., 0 g fiber, 47 g pro.
Daily Values: 19% vit. A, 16% vit. C, 16% calcium, 4% iron

Pistachio-Salmon Nuggets

You also can serve these chunks of salmon with toothpicks as an appetizer.

Prep: 15 minutes Marinate: 30 minutes Cook: 6 minutes Makes: 4 servings
- 1 pound fresh or frozen skinless salmon fillets, 1 inch thick
- 2 tablespoons water
- 2 tablespoons soy sauce
- 2 tablespoons cooking oil
- 1 tablespoon grated fresh ginger
- 1 tablespoon finely chopped pistachio nuts

1 Thaw fish, if frozen. Rinse fish; pat dry with paper towels. Cut fish into 1-inch chunks. Place fish in a self-sealing plastic bag set in a shallow dish. For marinade, combine water, soy sauce, 1 tablespoon of the oil, and ginger. Pour over fish; seal bag. Marinate at room temperature for 30 minutes, turning bag occasionally.

2 Drain fish, discarding marinade. In a large skillet cook and gently stir half of the fish chunks in the remaining 1 tablespoon hot oil for 3 to 5 minutes or until fish flakes easily when tested with a fork. Remove fish from skillet; place on paper towels. Cook and stir remaining fish; place on paper towels. Transfer fish to a serving platter; sprinkle with nuts.

Nutrition Facts per serving: 267 cal., 17 g total fat (3 g sat. fat), 70 mg chol., 514 mg sodium, 1 g carbo., 0 g fiber, 26 g pro.
Daily Values: 4% vit. A, 1% calcium, 3% iron

Orange-Onion Glazed Swordfish

Start to Finish: 20 minutes Makes: 4 servings
- 1   pound fresh or frozen swordfish steaks, 1 inch thick
- ¼ teaspoon salt
- ¼ teaspoon coarsely ground black pepper
  Nonstick cooking spray
- 1   tablespoon butter
- 1   large onion, thinly sliced and separated into rings (1 cup)
- ½ cup orange juice
- 1   tablespoon snipped fresh basil or 1 teaspoon dried basil, crushed

1 Thaw fish, if frozen. Rinse fish; pat dry with paper towels. Cut fish into 4 serving-size pieces. Sprinkle fish with salt and pepper.

2 Lightly coat a large skillet with cooking spray. Heat skillet over medium-high heat. Add swordfish to skillet. Cook, covered, about 12 minutes or until fish flakes easily when tested with a fork, turning once. Remove fish from skillet; keep warm.

3 Add butter to hot skillet. Cook and stir onion in hot butter until tender. Carefully stir in orange juice and basil. Bring to boiling; reduce heat. Simmer, uncovered, for 1 to 2 minutes or until most of the liquid has evaporated. Spoon onion mixture over fish.

Nutrition Facts per serving: 191 cal., 7 g total fat (3 g sat. fat), 51 mg chol., 280 mg sodium, 7 g carbo., 1 g fiber, 23 g pro.
Daily Values: 6% vit. A, 31% vit. C, 2% calcium, 6% iron

5
net carbs

Sweet Pepper and Salsa Fish

The pairing of salsa with mushrooms, sweet peppers, and onions gives this colorful dish a garden-fresh twist. If you like, garnish with sprigs of fresh oregano.

Start to Finish: 25 minutes Makes: 4 servings

- 1 pound fresh or frozen skinless fish fillets, ¾ inch thick
  Nonstick cooking spray
- 1½ cups fresh mushrooms, sliced
- 1 cup coarsely chopped green and/or yellow sweet pepper
- 1 small onion, halved lengthwise and sliced
- 1 cup bottled salsa

1 Thaw fish, if frozen. Rinse fish; pat dry with paper towels. Cut fish into 4 serving-size pieces; set aside.

2 Lightly coat a large nonstick skillet with cooking spray. Cook mushrooms, sweet pepper, and onion in skillet over medium-high heat about 5 minutes or until tender. Remove vegetables with a slotted spoon; set aside.

3 Reduce heat to medium. Add fish to the skillet. Cook, covered, for 6 to 9 minutes or until the fish flakes easily when tested with a fork, turning once.

4 Spoon cooked vegetables over fish in skillet; top with salsa. Cook, covered, over low heat about 2 minutes more or until heated through.

Nutrition Facts per serving: 108 cal., 1 g total fat (0 g sat. fat), 22 mg chol., 213 mg sodium, 7 g carbo., 2 g fiber, 18 g pro. Daily Values: 10% vit. A, 57% vit. C, 5% calcium, 5% iron

Salmon with Dijon-Cream Sauce

If you can't find butter with garlic, cook a clove of minced garlic in 1 tablespoon plain butter before adding the salmon slices to the skillet.

Start to Finish: 25 minutes Makes: 4 servings
- 1¼ pounds fresh or frozen skinless salmon fillets
- 1 tablespoon butter with garlic
- ⅓ cup reduced-sodium chicken broth
- ⅓ cup half-and-half or light cream
- 2 tablespoons Dijon-style mustard
- ¼ teaspoon coarsely ground black pepper

1 Thaw salmon, if frozen. Rinse fish; pat dry with paper towels. Cut fillets crosswise into ½-inch slices. In a large skillet cook salmon slices, half at a time, in hot butter over medium-high heat about 2 minutes or until fish flakes easily when tested with a fork, turning once. Remove from skillet; keep warm.

2 For sauce, add chicken broth to drippings in skillet. Bring to boiling; reduce heat. Simmer, uncovered, for 1 minute. Whisk together half-and-half and mustard; stir into skillet. Return to boiling; reduce heat. Simmer, uncovered, for 2 to 3 minutes more or until sauce is slightly thickened. Spoon sauce over salmon; sprinkle with pepper.

Nutrition Facts per serving: 318 cal., 20 g total fat (6 g sat. fat), 95 mg chol., 343 mg sodium, 1 g carbo., 0 g fiber, 29 g pro.
Daily Values: 4% vit. A, 8% vit. C, 4% calcium, 3% iron

3
net carbs

Chilled Cod with Gazpacho Sauce

Two summertime favorites—chilled poached fish and gazpacho—combine to make this refreshing dish.

Prep: 25 minutes Chill: 2 to 4 hours Makes: 2 servings
- 8 ounces fresh or frozen cod, flounder, or orange roughy fillets
- 1 medium lemon, halved and sliced
- ¼ cup marinated cucumber salad from deli, drained
- ¼ cup bottled chunky salsa
- 2 cups torn mixed salad greens

1 Thaw fish, if frozen. Rinse fish; pat dry with paper towels. Measure thickness of fish. Fill a large skillet with water to a depth of ½ inch. Bring water to boiling; reduce heat. Meanwhile, place fish in steamer basket (if necessary, cut fish into 2 pieces to fit). Place half of the lemon slices on top of fish. Place steamer over simmering water. Cover and simmer gently until fish flakes easily when tested with a fork (allow 4 to 6 minutes per ½-inch thickness of fish). Discard lemon slices. Cover and chill fish for 2 to 4 hours.

2 For sauce, cut up any large pieces of the cucumber salad. Stir together salad and salsa. Arrange salad greens on 2 dinner plates. Top each with half of the chilled fish. Spoon sauce over fish. Garnish with remaining lemon slices.

Nutrition Facts per serving: 116 cal., 15 g total fat (0 g sat. fat), 49 mg chol., 343 mg sodium, 5 g carbo., 2 g fiber, 21 g pro.
Daily Values: 54% vit. A, 9% vit. C, 4% calcium, 4% iron

Lobster Tails with Chive Butter

With just 1 carb per serving, this luscious lobster tail cradled in its coral-color shell and served with melted butter gets a nod of approval from both carb-counters and non-carb-counters.

Prep: 10 minutes Grill: 12 minutes Makes: 4 servings
- 4 5-ounce fresh or frozen rock lobster tails
- ⅓ cup butter
- 2 tablespoons snipped fresh chives
- 1 teaspoon finely shredded lemon peel
- Lemon wedges (optional)

1 Thaw lobster, if frozen. Rinse lobster; pat dry with paper towels. Butterfly tails by using kitchen scissors or a sharp knife to cut lengthwise through centers of hard top shells and meat, cutting to, but not through, bottoms of shells. Press shell halves of tails apart with your fingers.

2 For sauce, in a small saucepan melt butter. Remove from heat. Stir in chives and lemon peel. Remove 2 tablespoons of the sauce for brushing lobster. Set aside the remaining sauce for dipping sauce. Brush lobster with some of the brushing sauce.

3 For a charcoal grill, grill lobster, meat sides down, on the greased rack of an uncovered grill directly over medium coals for 12 to 15 minutes or until lobster meat is opaque, turning once and brushing with remaining brushing sauce halfway through grilling. (For a gas grill, preheat grill. Reduce heat to medium. Place lobster tails meat sides down on the greased grill rack directly over heat. Cover and grill as above.)

4 Heat the reserved dipping sauce, stirring occasionally. Transfer the sauce to small bowls for dipping and serve with lobster. If desired, serve with lemon wedges.

Nutrition Facts per serving: 214 cal., 17 g total fat (10 g sat. fat), 118 mg chol., 395 mg sodium, 1 g carbo., 0 g fiber, 15 g pro.
Daily Values: 3% vit. C, 4% calcium, 1% iron

Coconut-Curry Shrimp

Start to Finish: 25 minutes Makes: 4 servings

- 1 pound fresh or frozen peeled, cooked large shrimp
- 1 13½-ounce can unsweetened coconut milk
- 1 to 3 teaspoons red curry paste
- 1 16-ounce package frozen loose-pack broccoli, green beans, pearl onions, and red peppers
- 2 tablespoons snipped fresh cilantro or chopped peanuts

1 Thaw shrimp, if frozen. Rinse shrimp; set aside. In a large skillet stir together coconut milk and red curry paste. Add vegetables. Bring to boiling; reduce heat. Simmer, covered, for 6 to 8 minutes or until vegetables are crisp-tender, stirring occasionally. Add shrimp; heat through. Sprinkle with cilantro.

Nutrition Facts per serving: 336 cal., 20 g total fat (16 g sat. fat), 172 mg chol., 306 mg sodium, 11 g carbo., 3 g fiber, 26 g pro. Daily Values: 15% vit. A, 42% vit. C, 6% calcium, 19% iron

Jerk-Spiced Shrimp with Wilted Spinach

To avoid overfilling the skillet, cook the spinach half at a time. Once the first portion has wilted, remove it from the skillet and arrange on the serving platter. Then cook the remaining spinach.

Start to Finish: 25 minutes Makes: 4 servings
- 12 ounces fresh or frozen peeled, deveined medium shrimp
- 1½ teaspoons Jamaican jerk seasoning
- 3 cloves garlic, minced
- 2 tablespoons olive oil
- 8 cups torn fresh spinach

1 Thaw shrimp, if frozen. Rinse shrimp; pat dry with paper towels. In a small bowl toss together shrimp and jerk seasoning; set aside.

2 In a large skillet cook garlic in 1 tablespoon of the hot oil for 15 to 30 seconds. Add half of the spinach. Cook and stir about 1 minute or until spinach is just wilted. Transfer to a serving platter. Repeat with remaining spinach. Cover; keep warm.

3 Carefully add the remaining 1 tablespoon oil to skillet. Add shrimp. Cook and stir for 2 to 3 minutes or until shrimp turn opaque. Spoon shrimp over wilted spinach.

Nutrition Facts per serving: 159 cal., 8 g total fat (1 g sat. fat), 129 mg chol., 315 mg sodium, 2 g carbo., 6 g fiber, 19 g pro. Daily Values: 70% vit. A, 28% vit. C, 10% calcium, 34% iron

Garlic-Buttered Shrimp

Busy cooks will savor this delightfully easy grilled version of scampi-style shrimp.

Prep: 20 minutes Grill: 6 minutes Makes: 4 servings
- 1 pound fresh or frozen large shrimp in shells
- 2 tablespoons butter
- 2 cloves garlic, minced
- 1 tablespoon snipped fresh parsley
  Dash cayenne pepper
- 2 tablespoons dry white wine

1 Thaw shrimp, if frozen. Peel and devein shrimp, keeping tails intact. Rinse shrimp; pat dry with paper towels. Thread shrimp onto 4 long metal skewers. Set aside.

2 For sauce, in a small saucepan melt butter. Stir in garlic, parsley, and cayenne pepper; cook for 1 minute. Stir in wine; heat through. Set sauce aside.

3 For a charcoal grill, grill kabobs on the greased grill rack of an uncovered grill directly over medium coals for 6 to 10 minutes or until shrimp turn opaque, turning once and brushing frequently with sauce. (For a gas grill, preheat grill. Reduce heat to medium. Place kabobs on greased grill rack over heat. Cover and grill as above.)

Nutrition Facts per serving: 159 cal., 8 g total fat (4 g sat. fat), 156 mg chol., 199 mg sodium, 1 g carbo., 0 g fiber, 19 g pro. Daily Values: 9% vit. A, 5% vit. C, 5% calcium, 13% iron

Shrimp and Scallop Skewers

For an eye-pleasing presentation, nestle the scallops in the curls of the shrimp when threading the skewers. Sea scallops are the large scallops and work best for kabobs.

Prep: 20 minutes Marinate: 30 minutes Grill: 5 minutes Makes: 4 servings
- 12 fresh or frozen medium shrimp in shells
- 12 large fresh or frozen sea scallops
- ⅔ cup bottled Italian salad dressing
- 2 medium sweet peppers, cut into 1½-inch pieces

1 Thaw shrimp and scallops, if frozen. Peel and devein shrimp. Rinse; pat dry with paper towels. Place shrimp and scallops in a self-sealing plastic bag set in a shallow dish. Pour ½ cup of the salad dressing over shrimp and scallops; seal bag. Marinate in refrigerator for 30 minutes to 2 hours, turning bag occasionally. Drain, discarding marinade.

2 Meanwhile, cook sweet pepper pieces in boiling water for 2 minutes; drain. Alternately thread shrimp, scallops, and sweet pepper pieces onto 8 long metal skewers.

3 For a charcoal grill, grill skewers on the greased rack of an uncovered grill directly over medium coals for 5 to 8 minutes or until shrimp and scallops turn opaque, turning once halfway through grilling. (For a gas grill, preheat grill. Reduce heat to medium. Place skewers on greased grill rack over heat. Cover and grill as above.) Just before serving, brush skewers with remaining salad dressing.

Nutrition Facts per serving: 174 cal., 8 g total fat (1 g sat. fat), 76 mg chol., 264 mg sodium, 7 g carbo., 1 g fiber, 18 g pro.
Daily Values: 66% vit. A, 163% vit. C, 4% calcium, 7% iron

Buttery Bay Scallops

Start to Finish: 10 minutes Makes: 3 or 4 servings

- 12 ounces fresh or frozen bay scallops
- 1 clove garlic, minced
- ⅛ teaspoon dried tarragon, crushed
- 2 tablespoons butter
-    Salt and black pepper

1 Thaw scallops, if frozen. Rinse scallops; pat dry with paper towels. In a large skillet cook garlic and tarragon in hot butter over medium heat for 1 minute. Remove skillet from heat. Add scallops to skillet; sprinkle with salt and pepper. Cook, stirring frequently, over medium-high heat for 2 to 3 minutes or until scallops turn opaque.

Nutrition Facts per serving: 173 cal., 9 g total fat (5 g sat. fat), 59 mg chol., 362 mg sodium, 3 g carbo., 0 g fiber, 19 g pro.
Daily Values: 7% vit. A, 5% vit. C, 3% calcium, 2% iron

Citus Scallops

Start to Finish: 15 minutes Makes: 4 servings
- 1   pound fresh or frozen sea scallops
- 1   medium orange
- 1   tablespoon olive oil
- 2   cloves garlic, minced
- ½   teaspoon snipped fresh thyme
-     Salt and black pepper

1 Thaw scallops, if frozen. Rinse scallops; pat dry with paper towels. Set scallops aside. Finely shred 1 teaspoon peel from the orange. Cut orange in half; squeeze until you have ⅓ cup juice.

2 Heat oil in a large skillet over medium-high heat. Add scallops. Cook, stirring frequently, for 2 to 3 minutes or until scallops turn opaque. Transfer scallops to a serving platter; keep warm.

3 For sauce, add garlic to skillet; cook and stir for 30 seconds (add more oil to skillet, if necessary). Add orange peel, orange juice, and thyme to skillet. Bring to boiling; reduce heat. Simmer, uncovered, for 1 to 2 minutes or until desired consistency. Season to taste with salt and pepper. Pour over scallops.

Nutrition Facts per serving: 142 cal., 4 g total fat (1 g sat. fat), 37 mg chol., 218 mg sodium, 5 g carbo., 0 g fiber, 19 g pro.
Daily Values: 2% vit. A, 24% vit. C, 3% calcium, 2% iron

Pan-Seared Scallops with Lemon Vinaigrette

Prep: 20 minutes Cook: 6 minutes Makes: 4 servings

- 12 ounces fresh or frozen sea scallops
- 1 lemon
- 1 pound asparagus spears, cut into 2-inch pieces
- 1 medium red onion, cut into wedges
- 3 tablespoons olive oil
  - Salt and black pepper
- 2 or 3 fresh basil sprigs

1 Thaw scallops, if frozen. Rinse scallops; pat dry with paper towels. Set scallops aside.

2 Score lemon into 4 lengthwise sections with a sharp knife; remove peel from lemon. Scrape off white portion from peel; discard. Cut peel into very thin strips; set aside. Squeeze 2 tablespoons juice from lemon; set juice aside.

3 In a large skillet cook asparagus and onion in 1 tablespoon of hot oil for 2 to 3 minutes or until crisp-tender. Season to taste with salt and pepper. Transfer asparagus mixture to a serving platter; keep warm.

4 In the same skillet combine the reserved lemon peel, the remaining 2 tablespoons oil, and basil sprigs. Cook for 30 seconds to 1 minute or until heated through. Remove lemon peel and basil sprigs with a slotted spoon, reserving oil in skillet. Discard lemon peel and basil.

5 Cook scallops in the hot flavored oil for 3 to 5 minutes or until scallops turn opaque, turning once. Stir in the reserved lemon juice. Season to taste with salt and pepper. Arrange scallops over asparagus mixture.

Nutrition Facts per serving: 190 cal., 11 g total fat (1 g sat. fat), 28 mg chol., 147 mg sodium, 6 g carbo., 1 g fiber, 16 g pro. Daily Values: 36% vit. C, 3% calcium, 4% iron

chapter 4

Eggs and Cheese

net carbs

Stuffed Eggs with Salmon and Dill

The filling for these deviled eggs is extra creamy, thanks to sour cream dip. Lox-style salmon and fresh dill make tasty toppers.

Prep: 25 minutes Stand: 15 minutes Cool: 15 minutes Makes: 12 servings

    6 hard-cooked eggs
    ¼ cup dairy sour cream dill or chive dip
    ½ teaspoon finely shredded lemon peel
       Salt and black pepper
    1 ounce smoked salmon (lox-style), cut into bite-size strips
       Snipped fresh dill or chives (optional)

1 Halve hard-cooked eggs lengthwise and remove yolks. Set whites aside. Place yolks in a bowl; mash with a fork. Add sour cream dip and lemon peel; mix well. Season to taste with salt and pepper. Stuff egg white halves with yolk mixture. Top eggs with strips of smoked salmon. If desired, garnish with dill.

✳Note: To hard cook eggs, place eggs in a single layer in a saucepan. Add enough cold water to just cover the eggs. Bring to a rapid boil over high heat (water will have large, rapidly breaking bubbles). Remove from heat, cover, and let stand for 15 minutes; drain. Run cold water over eggs or place them in ice water until cool enough to handle; drain. To peel eggs, gently tap each egg on the countertop. Roll the egg between the palms of your hands. Peel off eggshell, starting at the large end.

Nutrition Facts per serving: 52 cal., 3 g total fat (1 g sat. fat), 107 mg chol., 122 mg sodium, 1 g carbo., 0 g fiber, 4 g pro.
Daily Values: 3% vit. A, 1% calcium, 2% iron

Decadent Deviled Eggs

Deviled eggs take a fancier stance with the addition of crab. Be sure to use real crabmeat because imitation crabmeat contains added carbohydrates.

Start to Finish: 20 minutes   Makes: 12 servings

- 6 hard-cooked eggs (see note, page 122)
- 1/3 cup mayonnaise
- 2 teaspoons Dijon-style mustard
- 1 teaspoon snipped fresh chives
- 1 6- to 6½-ounce can crabmeat, drained, flaked, and cartilage removed
   Salt and black pepper (optional)
   Fresh chives (optional)

1 Halve hard-cooked eggs lengthwise and remove yolks. Set whites aside. Place yolks in a bowl; mash with a fork. Add mayonnaise, mustard, and the 1 teaspoon chives; mix well. Gently stir in crabmeat. If desired, season to taste with salt and pepper.

2 Stuff egg white halves with crab mixture. If desired, garnish with additional chives.

Nutrition Facts per serving: 98 cal., 8 g total fat (2 g sat. fat), 121 mg chol., 130 mg sodium, 0 g carbo., 0 g fiber, 6 g pro.
Daily Values: 3% vit. A, 1% vit. C, 3% calcium, 2% iron

Meat Lover's Scrambled Eggs

This hearty breakfast features a popular trio of meats—bacon, sausage, and ham.

Start to Finish: 20 minutes Makes: 4 servings

- 8 eggs
- ½ cup water
- ¼ teaspoon salt
- ⅛ teaspoon black pepper
- 4 slices bacon, chopped
- 4 ounces bulk pork sausage
- ½ cup chopped cooked ham and/or Polish sausage
- ½ cup shredded cheddar cheese
- Thinly sliced green onion (optional)

1 In a medium bowl beat together eggs, water, salt, and pepper with a fork or rotary beater; set aside.

2 In a large skillet cook and stir bacon and sausage over medium heat until bacon is crisp and pork is no longer pink. Drain, reserving 1 tablespoon drippings in skillet. Set bacon and sausage aside.

3 Add egg mixture to drippings in skillet. Cook over medium heat, without stirring, until mixture begins to set on the bottom and around edge. Sprinkle bacon, sausage, and ham over egg mixture.

4 With a spatula or a large spoon, lift and fold the partially cooked egg mixture so the uncooked portion flows underneath. Continue cooking over medium heat for 2 to 3 minutes or until egg mixture is cooked through but is still glossy and moist. Sprinkle with shredded cheese and, if desired, green onion. Remove from heat immediately. Let stand 1 to 2 minutes or until cheese melts.

Nutrition Facts per serving: 380 cal., 29 g total fat (11 g sat. fat), 473 mg chol., 707 mg sodium, 2 g carbo., 0 g fiber, 25 g pro.
Daily Values: 16% vit. A, 16% calcium, 11% iron

Scrambled Eggs with Sausage and Feta

Stir the feta cheese into the scrambled eggs and sausage just a minute or 2 before the eggs are done. The cheese cooks just long enough to become warm and soft, creating tangy pockets of flavor in the eggs.

Start to Finish: 20 minutes Makes: 4 servings

- 8 eggs or 2 cups refrigerated or frozen egg product, thawed
- ½ cup milk
- 6 ounces smoked turkey sausage, sliced or chopped
- 2 tablespoons butter
- 1 4-ounce package crumbled feta cheese with garlic and herbs

1 In a medium bowl beat together eggs and milk with a fork or rotary beater; set aside.

2 In a large nonstick skillet cook sausage in hot butter over medium heat for 2 to 3 minutes or until sausage just begins to brown. Pour in egg mixture. Cook over medium heat, without stirring, until mixture begins to set on the bottom and around edge.

3 With a spatula or a large spoon, lift and fold the partially cooked egg mixture so the uncooked portion flows underneath. When eggs are almost set, sprinkle with feta cheese. Continue cooking over medium heat for 1 to 2 minutes or until egg mixture is cooked through but is still glossy and moist. Remove from heat.

Nutrition Facts per serving: 356 cal., 26 g total fat (12 g sat. fat), 497 mg chol., 889 mg sodium, 5 g carbo., 0 g fiber, 24 g pro.
Daily Values: 21% vit. A, 1% vit. C, 23% calcium, 12% iron

Scrambled Eggs with Salmon and Chives

Start to Finish: 15 minutes Makes: 4 servings

    6 eggs
    ⅓ cup water
    3 tablespoons snipped fresh chives
    1 tablespoon butter
    1 3- to 4-ounce package thinly sliced, smoked salmon (lox-style), cut into bite-size strips

1 In a medium bowl beat together eggs, water, and chives with a fork or rotary beater. In a large skillet melt butter over medium heat; pour in egg mixture. Cook over medium heat, without stirring, until mixture begins to set on the bottom and around edge.

2 With a spatula or large spoon, lift and fold partially cooked egg mixture so the uncooked portion flows underneath. Fold in salmon; continue cooking over medium heat for 2 to 3 minutes or until egg mixture is cooked through but is still glossy and moist.

Nutrition Facts per serving: 164 cal., 11 g total fat (4 g sat. fat), 332 mg chol., 551 mg sodium, 1 g carbo., 0 g fiber, 13 g pro. Daily Values: 13% vit. A, 1% vit. C, 4% calcium, 7% iron

Shrimp and Spinach Scrambled Eggs

Start to Finish: 20 minutes   Makes: 4 servings

8	ounces fresh or frozen peeled, deveined shrimp
8	eggs
½	cup milk
¼	teaspoon salt
¼	teaspoon black pepper
	Nonstick cooking spray
2½	cups fresh baby spinach
1	5-ounce container semisoft cheese with garlic and herb, crumbled

1 Thaw shrimp, if frozen. Rinse shrimp; pat dry with paper towels. Halve shrimp lengthwise; set aside.

2 In a medium bowl beat together eggs, milk, salt, and pepper with a fork or rotary beater; set aside.

3 Lightly coat a large nonstick skillet with cooking spray. Heat skillet over medium heat. Add shrimp and spinach to skillet; cook and stir for 2 to 3 minutes or until shrimp turn opaque.

4 Pour egg mixture into skillet. Cook over medium heat, without stirring, until mixture begins to set on the bottom and around edge. With a spatula or a large spoon, lift and fold the partially cooked egg mixture so the uncooked portion flows underneath. Continue cooking over medium heat for 2 to 3 minutes or until egg mixture is cooked through but is still glossy and moist.

5 Remove from heat; immediately sprinkle with cheese. Let stand 3 to 4 minutes or until cheese melts.

Nutrition Facts per serving: 343 cal., 23 g total fat (11 g sat. fat), 525 mg chol., 228 mg sodium, 4 g carbo., 2 g fiber, 25 g pro.
Daily Values: 36% vit. A, 9% vit. C, 14% calcium, 21% iron

0
net carbs

Spinach and Feta Omelet

Omelets are truly versatile. You can serve them for breakfast, lunch, or dinner. This Greek-inspired omelet is flecked with spinach and filled with crumbled feta.

Start to Finish: 25 minutes Makes: 1 serving
- 2 cups chopped fresh spinach
- 3 eggs
- 1 tablespoon butter
- ¼ cup crumbled feta cheese (1 ounce)

1 In a medium saucepan cook spinach, covered, in a small amount of boiling, salted water for 3 to 4 minutes or until tender. Drain spinach thoroughly.

2 In a medium bowl use a fork to beat eggs well. Add drained spinach; continue beating until combined.

3 Heat an 8-inch skillet with flared sides over medium-high heat until a drop of water sizzles. Add the butter to skillet. When butter has melted, pour egg mixture into skillet. Reduce heat to medium. As egg mixture sets, run a spatula around the edge of skillet, lifting cooked eggs so uncooked portion flows underneath. Cook until top of omelet is set but still shiny. Turn omelet; sprinkle with cheese. Cook 2 minutes more. Transfer omelet to a warm plate. Loosely roll or fold the omelet.

Nutrition Facts per serving: 357 cal., 27 g total fat (13 g sat. fat), 679 mg chol., 639 mg sodium, 3 g carbo., 6 g fiber, 25 g pro. Daily Values: 94% vit. A, 25% vit. C, 26% calcium, 37% iron

Sweet Pepper-Gruyère Omelet

Start to Finish: 10 minutes Makes: 1 serving
- ⅓ cup chopped red and/or green sweet pepper
- 1 tablespoon butter
- 2 eggs
- 2 tablespoons water
- Dash salt and black pepper
- ¼ cup shredded Gruyère or Swiss cheese (1 ounce)

1 In an 8-inch nonstick skillet with flared sides cook sweet pepper in hot butter over medium heat until tender. Remove sweet pepper from skillet with a slotted spoon; set aside.

2 Meanwhile, in a small bowl beat together eggs, water, salt, and pepper with a fork until combined but not frothy.

3 Add egg mixture to the hot skillet. Immediately begin stirring egg mixture gently but continuously with a wooden spoon or plastic spatula until mixture resembles small pieces of cooked egg surrounded by liquid egg. Stop stirring. Cook 30 to 60 seconds more or until egg mixture is set but shiny. Sprinkle cheese across center of omelet. Spoon cooked sweet peppers over cheese. With a spatula lift and fold an edge of the omelet about a third of the way toward the center. Remove from heat. Fold the opposite edge toward the center. Transfer to a warm plate.

Nutrition Facts per serving: 387 cal., 31 g total fat (16 g sat. fat), 489 mg chol., 487 mg sodium, 5 g carbo., 1 g fiber, 22 g pro. Daily Values: 82% vit. A, 132% vit. C, 34% calcium, 10% iron

3 net carbs

Puffy Omelet with Cheesy Chicken Filling

Be sure to use a skillet that can withstand the heat of the oven. A cast-iron skillet does the job nicely.

Start to Finish: 25 minutes Oven: 350°F Makes: 2 servings

- 4 egg whites
- ¼ teaspoon salt
- ⅛ teaspoon black pepper
- 2 tablespoons water
- 4 beaten egg yolks
- 1 tablespoon butter
- ⅔ cup shredded Monterey Jack cheese with jalapeño peppers or cheddar cheese
- 1 6-ounce package refrigerated cooked southwestern-style chicken breast strips, chopped
- 2 tablespoons salsa or picante sauce
  Salsa or picante sauce (optional)

1 In a medium mixing bowl beat egg whites, salt, and pepper with an electric mixer on medium to high speed until frothy. Add water; continue beating for 1 to 2 minutes or until stiff peaks form (tips stand straight). Fold in yolks.

2 In a large ovenproof skillet heat butter over medium-high heat until a drop of water sizzles. Spread egg mixture in skillet. Cook about 3 minutes or just until bottom is golden. Bake in a 350° oven for 3 to 4 minutes or until dry on top and edges are light brown.

3 Loosen the omelet from the sides of the skillet with a metal spatula. Make a shallow cut slightly off center across the omelet. Sprinkle cheese over the larger side. Top with chicken and the 2 tablespoons salsa. Fold smaller side of omelet over larger side. Cut omelet in half. If desired, serve with additional salsa.

Nutrition Facts per serving: 464 cal., 31 g total fat (16 g sat. fat), 537 mg chol., 1,540 mg sodium, 3 g carbo., 0 g fiber, 41 g pro. Daily Values: 29% vit. A, 2% vit. C, 32% calcium, 13% iron

French Omelet

Start to Finish: 7 minutes Makes: 1 serving
- 2 eggs
- 1 tablespoon water
- ⅛ teaspoon salt
- Dash black pepper
- Nonstick cooking spray

1 In a small bowl combine eggs, water, salt, and pepper. Beat with a fork or rotary beater until combined but not frothy. Lightly coat an unheated 8- or 10-inch nonstick skillet with flared sides with cooking spray.

2 Heat skillet over medium-high heat until skillet is hot. Add egg mixture to skillet; lower heat to medium. As eggs set, run a spatula around the edge of the skillet, lifting eggs so uncooked portion flows underneath. When eggs are set but still shiny, remove from heat. Fold omelet in half. Transfer to a warm plate.

Nutrition Facts per serving: 152 cal., 11 g total fat (3 g sat. fat), 426 mg chol., 393 mg sodium, 1 g carbo., 0 g fiber, 13 g pro. Daily Values: 19% vit. A, 4% vit. C, 9% iron

Mushroom Omelet: For filling, cook ⅓ cup sliced fresh mushrooms in 1 teaspoon butter until tender. Remove from skillet; keep warm. Prepare omelet as above. When eggs are set but still shiny, spoon filling across center of omelet. Fold sides of omelet over filling.

Per serving: 2 g carbo. and 0 g dietary fiber. Net Carbs: 2 g

Cheese Omelet: Prepare as above, except omit salt. When eggs are set but still shiny, sprinkle ¼ cup shredded cheddar, Swiss, or Monterey Jack cheese across center of omelet. Fold sides of omelet over cheese.

Per serving: 2 g carbo. and 0 g dietary fiber. Net Carbs: 2 g

2
net carbs

Turkey-Filled Puffy Omelet

Start to Finish: 25 minutes Oven: 350°F Makes: 2 servings
- 3 egg whites
  - Dash salt and black pepper
- 3 beaten egg yolks
  - Nonstick cooking spray
- 1 ounce semisoft goat cheese (chèvre), crumbled, or cream cheese, cut up
- 2 to 2½ ounces thinly sliced smoked turkey or cooked ham
- 1 tablespoon snipped fresh parsley

1 In a medium mixing bowl beat egg whites, salt, and pepper with an electric mixer on medium to high speed until stiff peaks form (tips stand straight). Fold in yolks.

2 Lightly coat a large ovenproof skillet with cooking spray. Heat skillet over medium-high heat. Spread egg mixture in skillet. Cook about 3 minutes or just until bottom is golden. Bake in a 350° oven 3 minutes or until dry on top and edges are light brown.

3 Loosen the omelet from the sides of the skillet with a metal spatula. Make a shallow cut slightly off center across the omelet. Sprinkle cheese over the larger side. Top with turkey and parsley. Fold smaller side of omelet over larger side. Cut omelet in half.

Nutrition Facts per serving: 183 cal., 11 g total fat (5 g sat. fat), 400 mg chol., 504 mg sodium, 2 g carbo., 0 g fiber, 18 g pro.
Daily Values: 12% vit. A, 4% vit. C, 6% calcium, 9% iron

Oven Omelets with Artichokes and Spinach

Start to Finish: 25 minutes Oven: 400°F Makes: 6 servings

    Nonstick cooking spray
- 10 eggs
- ¼ cup water
- ½ teaspoon salt
- ¼ teaspoon black pepper
- 2 6-ounce jars marinated artichoke hearts, drained and chopped
- 4 cups chopped fresh spinach
- ¾ cup shredded Swiss or provolone cheese (3 ounces)

1 Coat a 15×10×1-inch baking pan with cooking spray; set pan aside.

2 In a medium bowl beat together eggs, water, salt, and pepper with a fork or rotary beater until combined but not frothy.

3 Place the prepared pan on an oven rack. Carefully pour the egg mixture into the pan. Bake in a 400° oven about 7 minutes or until egg mixture is set but still has a glossy surface.

4 Meanwhile, for filling, in a large skillet cook artichoke hearts over medium heat until heated through, stirring occasionally. Add spinach; cook and stir until spinach is wilted.

5 Cut the baked egg mixture into six 5-inch square omelets. Remove omelet squares from pan using a large spatula. Invert omelet squares onto warm serving plates.

6 Spoon filling on half of each omelet square. Sprinkle with cheese. Fold the other omelet half over the filled half, forming a triangle or rectangle.

Nutrition Facts per serving: 225 cal., 16 g total fat (5 g sat. fat), 367 mg chol., 342 mg sodium, 7 g carbo., 2 g fiber, 16 g pro.
Daily Values: 35% vit. A, 30% vit. C, 20% calcium, 17% iron

4

net carbs

Baked Omelets with Pesto Vegetables

Start to Finish: 35 minutes Oven: 400°F Makes: 6 servings

- Nonstick cooking spray
- 3 cups refrigerated or frozen egg product, thawed, or 12 eggs
- ¼ cup water
- ⅛ teaspoon salt
- ⅛ teaspoon black pepper
- 2 cups desired frozen vegetables
- 3 tablespoons purchased basil pesto

1 Coat a 15×10×1-inch baking pan with cooking spray; set pan aside.

2 In a medium bowl beat together egg product, water, salt, and pepper with a fork or rotary beater until combined but not frothy. Place prepared pan on center oven rack. Pour egg mixture into pan. Bake, uncovered, in a 400° oven about 8 minutes or until mixture is set but still has a glossy surface.

3 Meanwhile, cook the frozen vegetables according to package directions; drain. Cut up any large vegetable pieces; stir in pesto.

4 Cut baked eggs into six 5-inch squares. Remove omelet squares from pan using a large spatula. Invert omelet squares onto warm serving plates. Spoon about ¼ cup of the cooked vegetables on half of each omelet square. Fold the other omelet half over the filled half, forming a triangle or rectangle.

Nutrition Facts per serving: 142 cal., 7 g total fat (2 g sat. fat), 4 mg chol., 290 mg sodium, 5 g carbo., 1 g fiber, 15 g pro.
Daily Values: 15% vit. A, 9% vit. C, 11% calcium, 15% iron

Broccoli Omelet Provençal

Steamed broccoli slaw enhanced with fresh oregano fills these easy-to-make oven omelets. Add a spoonful of warmed pasta sauce for a delicious, colorful touch.

Start to Finish: 20 minutes Oven: 400°F Makes: 6 servings

	Nonstick cooking spray
12	eggs
¼	cup water
½	teaspoon garlic salt
⅛	teaspoon black pepper
3	cups packaged shredded broccoli (broccoli slaw mix)
2	tablespoons snipped fresh oregano or basil
1¼	cups light no-sugar-added pasta sauce, warmed

1 Lightly coat a 15×10×1-inch baking pan with cooking spray; set aside. In a medium bowl beat together eggs, water, garlic salt, and pepper with a fork or rotary beater until combined but not frothy.

2 Place the prepared baking pan on an oven rack. Carefully pour egg mixture into the pan. Bake in a 400° oven about 7 minutes or until egg mixture is set but is still glossy and moist.

3 Meanwhile, for filling, place a steamer basket in a medium saucepan. Add water to just below bottom of basket. Bring to boiling. Add broccoli to steamer basket. Steam, covered, for 2 to 3 minutes or until heated through; drain well. Stir in oregano.

4 Cut the baked egg mixture into six 5-inch squares. Remove omelet squares from pan using a large spatula. Invert omelet squares onto warm serving plates. Spoon filling on half of each omelet square. Fold the other omelet half over the filled half, forming a triangle or rectangle. Spoon warm pasta sauce over omelets.

Nutrition Facts per serving: 183 cal., 11 g total fat (3 g sat. fat), 425 mg chol., 364 mg sodium, 7 g carbo., 2 g fiber, 15 g pro. Daily Values: 30% vit. A, 72% vit. C, 10% calcium, 13% iron

Pepperoni Pizza Frittata

If you find yourself craving pizza now and then, try this frittata. Topped with roma tomatoes, pepperoni, and melted mozzarella, it looks and tastes like pizza.

Start to Finish: 30 minutes Makes: 4 servings

Nonstick cooking spray
- 6 slightly beaten eggs
- ¾ teaspoon dried oregano, crushed
- ¼ teaspoon salt
- ¼ teaspoon black pepper
- ¾ cup chopped roma tomatoes
- ⅓ cup chopped pepperoni
- ½ cup shredded mozzarella cheese (2 ounces)

1 Lightly coat a large broiler-proof skillet with cooking spray. Heat skillet over medium heat.

2 Meanwhile, in a medium bowl beat together eggs, oregano, salt, and pepper with a fork or rotary beater. Pour egg mixture into skillet. As mixture sets, run a spatula around edge of skillet, lifting egg mixture so uncooked portion flows underneath. Continue cooking and lifting edges until almost set (surface will be moist).

3 Remove skillet from heat. Sprinkle with chopped tomatoes. Place skillet under the broiler 4 to 5 inches from heat. Broil 1 to 2 minutes or just until top is set. Remove from broiler; top with pepperoni and cheese. Return to broiler. Broil 1 to 2 minutes more or until cheese is melted.

Nutrition Facts per serving: 212 cal., 15 g total fat (6 g sat. fat), 338 mg chol., 512 mg sodium, 3 g carbo., 1 g fiber, 15 g pro. Daily Values: 16% vit. A, 11% vit. C, 12% calcium, 9% iron

Smoked Salmon Frittata

Start to Finish: 25 minutes Makes: 4 servings

- 6 eggs
- ¼ teaspoon black pepper
  Nonstick cooking spray
- ¼ cup sliced green onions
- 1 4-ounce piece smoked salmon, flaked, with skin and bones removed
- 2 tablespoons snipped fresh dill or 1 teaspoon dried dill
- 1 ounce semisoft goat cheese (chèvre), crumbled

1 In a medium bowl beat together eggs and pepper with a fork or rotary beater; set aside.

2 Lightly coat a large broiler-proof skillet with cooking spray. Cook onions in skillet over medium heat until tender. Stir in salmon and dill. Pour egg mixture into skillet over salmon. As mixture sets, run a spatula around edge of skillet, lifting egg mixture so the uncooked portion flows underneath. Continue cooking and lifting edges until almost set (surface will be moist).

3 Place skillet under the broiler 4 to 5 inches from the heat. Broil for 1 to 2 minutes or until top is just set. Sprinkle with cheese.

Nutrition Facts per serving: 166 cal., 10 g total fat (4 g sat. fat), 329 mg chol., 344 mg sodium, 1 g carbo., 0 g fiber, 16 g pro.
Daily Values: 11% vit. A, 2% vit. C, 6% calcium, 9% iron

Leek and Carrot Frittata

Start to Finish: 30 minutes Makes: 4 servings

- 8 eggs
- ½ teaspoon salt
- ¼ teaspoon black pepper
- 2 tablespoons olive oil
- 1 cup sliced leek
- ⅔ cup packaged shredded carrot
- ¼ cup finely shredded Parmesan cheese

1 In a medium bowl beat together eggs, salt, and pepper with a fork or rotary beater; set aside. In a large broiler-proof skillet heat oil over medium heat. Add leek; cook and stir for 4 minutes. Add carrot; cook and stir about 2 minutes more or until vegetables are crisp-tender.

2 Pour egg mixture over vegetables. As mixture sets, run a spatula around edge of skillet, lifting egg mixture so uncooked portion flows underneath. Continue cooking and lifting edges until almost set. Remove skillet from heat. Sprinkle with Parmesan cheese. Place skillet under broiler 4 to 5 inches from heat. Broil 2 to 3 minutes or until top is set and just beginning to brown.

Nutrition Facts per serving: 370 cal., 26 g total fat (10 g sat. fat), 449 mg chol., 993 mg sodium, 8 g carbo., 1 g fiber, 26 g pro. Daily Values: 132% vit. A, 8% vit. C, 49% calcium, 13% iron

Crustless Mexican Quiche

A quiche minus the crust, such as this Mexican-inspired version, makes a delicious low-carb lunch or light supper. Chorizo and Monterey Jack cheese with jalapeños add the Mexican touches.

Prep: 15 minutes Bake: 30 minutes Stand: 10 minutes Oven: 325°F Makes: 6 servings

   Nonstick cooking spray
 8 ounces bulk chorizo or hot pork sausage
 4 beaten eggs
1½ cups half-and-half or light cream
1½ cups shredded Monterey Jack cheese with jalapeño peppers
 ⅓ cup bottled salsa

1 Lightly coat a 9-inch pie plate with cooking spray; set aside.

2 In a small skillet cook chorizo until brown; drain off fat. Meanwhile, in a medium bowl stir together eggs and half-and-half; stir in cooked chorizo. Add cheese; mix well. Pour egg mixture into prepared pie plate.

3 Bake in a 325° oven about 30 minutes or until a knife inserted near center comes out clean. Let stand 10 minutes before serving. Top each serving with salsa.

Nutrition Facts per serving: 406 cal., 33 g total fat (16 g sat. fat), 222 mg chol., 714 mg sodium, 4 g carbo., 0 g fiber, 22 g pro.
Daily Values: 16% vit. A, 3% vit. C, 29% calcium, 8% iron

Cheesy Vegetable Baked Eggs

Unless you're a pro at cracking eggs, break each egg into a custard cup or small bowl before slipping it into the cooked vegetables. This way you'll avoid getting any broken yolks or bits of shell in the finished dish.

Prep: 20 minutes Bake: 20 minutes Stand: 5 minutes Oven: 350°F Makes: 4 servings

- 2 tablespoons butter
- 2 cups assorted fresh vegetables (such as chopped sweet pepper, sliced button mushrooms, seeded and chopped tomatoes, chopped green onion, and/or chopped zucchini)
- ¼ teaspoon salt
- ⅛ teaspoon black pepper
- 8 eggs
- ¾ teaspoon snipped fresh dill or 1 tablespoon snipped fresh chives or parsley
- ⅔ cup shredded Swiss, smoked mozzarella, or smoked cheddar cheese

1 In a medium skillet melt 1 tablespoon of the butter over medium heat. Add desired vegetables. Cook and stir for 3 to 4 minutes or until vegetables are tender. Sprinkle with salt and pepper; set vegetables aside.

2 Grease a 3-quart rectangular baking dish with the remaining 1 tablespoon butter. Spread cooked vegetable mixture evenly over the bottom of the prepared pan. Carefully break eggs into pan on top of vegetables. Sprinkle with dill and, if desired, additional salt and pepper.

3 Bake, covered, in a 350° oven about 20 minutes or until egg whites are opaque and yolks are firm. Sprinkle cheese over eggs. Cover and let stand about 5 minutes or until cheese is melted.

Nutrition Facts per serving: 290 cal., 22 g total fat (10 g sat. fat), 458 mg chol., 231 mg sodium, 5 g carbo., 1 g fiber, 19 g pro.
Daily Values: 46% vit. A, 69% vit. C, 26% calcium, 10% iron

Breakfast Bake

Put all your eggs in one dish—along with ham and your favorite cheese, such as cheddar, Swiss, or American.

Prep: 20 minutes Chill: 2 to 24 hours Bake: 35 minutes Stand: 10 minutes Oven: 325°F
Makes: 6 servings

Nonstick cooking spray
6 slices low-carb bread
1 2½-ounce package very thinly sliced cooked ham, cut into bite-size pieces (½ cup)
½ cup shredded cheddar, Swiss, or American cheese (2 ounces)
6 eggs
1¼ cups milk
⅛ teaspoon black pepper

1 Coat a 2-quart rectangular baking dish with cooking spray. Tear bread into bite-size pieces. Sprinkle half of the bread pieces into the bottom of the baking dish.

2 Sprinkle ham and cheese over bread in baking dish. Sprinkle remaining torn bread over ham and cheese.

3 In a medium bowl combine eggs, milk, and pepper. Mix with a rotary beater or fork until combined. Pour egg mixture over bread in the baking dish. Cover and chill for 2 to 24 hours.

4 Bake, uncovered, in a 325° oven for 35 to 40 minutes or until a knife inserted in center comes out clean. Let stand 10 minutes. Cut into squares to serve.

Nutrition Facts per serving: 219 cal., 12 g total fat (5 g sat. fat), 233 mg chol., 372 mg sodium, 15 g carbo., 8 g fiber, 19 g pro.
Daily Values: 15% vit. A, 1% vit. C, 26% calcium, 15% iron

Brunch Portobellos

Prep: 15 minutes Bake: 15 minutes Oven: 350°F Makes: 4 servings
- 4 fresh portobello mushrooms (3 to 5 ounces each)
- 4 eggs
- 3 tablespoons water
- ⅛ teaspoon salt
-    Dash black pepper
-    Nonstick cooking spray
- 2 tablespoons sliced green onion (1)
- 2 tablespoons roasted red sweet peppers, drained and chopped

1 Clean and remove stems from mushrooms. Place mushroom caps stemmed sides up in an ungreased shallow baking pan. Bake, uncovered, in a 350° oven for 15 to 20 minutes or until tender.

2 Meanwhile, in a medium bowl beat together eggs, water, salt, and pepper with a rotary beater; set egg mixture aside. Lightly coat a large nonstick skillet with cooking spray. Heat skillet over medium heat. Add green onion to skillet. Cook and stir for 30 seconds. Pour in egg mixture. Cook over medium heat, without stirring, until mixture begins to set on the bottom and around edge.

3 With a spatula or large spoon, lift and fold partially cooked egg mixture so the uncooked portion flows underneath. Continue cooking over medium heat for 2 to 3 minutes or until egg mixture is cooked through but is still glossy and moist. Remove from heat. Fill mushrooms with scrambled eggs; top with roasted peppers.

Nutrition Facts per serving: 106 cal., 5 g total fat (2 g sat. fat), 213 mg chol., 143 mg sodium, 7 g carbo., 2 g fiber, 9 g pro. Daily Values: 7% vit. A, 22% vit. C, 4% calcium, 8% iron

Cheese-Stuffed Eggplant Sandwiches

You'll need a knife and fork to eat these hot-from-the-oven sandwiches. Tomato slices and a feta-cottage cheese spread are sandwiched between eggplant slices and baked in the oven.

Prep: 15 minutes Bake: 25 minutes Oven: 450°F Makes: 4 servings
- 1 medium eggplant (about 1 pound)
- 2 tablespoons olive oil
- 1 4-ounce package crumbled feta cheese with garlic and herbs
- ½ cup low-fat cottage cheese
- 3 roma tomatoes, cut into ¼-inch slices

1 Wash eggplant; peel, if desired. Cut eggplant crosswise into sixteen ¼-inch slices. Set aside.

2 Brush a 15×10×1-inch baking pan with 1 tablespoon of the olive oil. Place half of the eggplant slices in the prepared pan.

3 In a small bowl stir together ½ cup of the feta cheese and the cottage cheese. Spoon cheese mixture evenly onto the eggplant slices in pan; top with tomato slices and the remaining eggplant slices. Brush top of eggplant slices with the remaining oil.

4 Bake in a 450° oven for 20 to 25 minutes or until eggplant is nearly tender. Top with remaining feta cheese. Bake for 5 minutes more.

Nutrition Facts per serving: 167 cal., 10 g total fat (5 g sat. fat), 26 mg chol., 436 mg sodium, 12 g carbo., 4 g fiber, 9 g pro.
Daily Values: 12% vit. A, 23% vit. C, 17% calcium, 5% iron

Portobellos Florentine

Prep: 15 minutes Bake: 20 minutes Oven: 350°F Makes: 4 servings
- 4 portobello mushrooms (about 5 inches in diameter)
- ½ cup purchased basil pesto
- 1 cup finely chopped fresh spinach leaves or half of a 10-ounce package frozen chopped spinach, thawed and well drained
- ½ cup ricotta cheese
- 2 medium roma tomatoes, chopped

1 Remove stems from mushrooms, if present (discard stems). Spread stem sides of mushroom caps with ¼ cup of the pesto. Place caps stem sides up in a shallow baking pan.

2 In a small bowl combine the remaining ¼ cup pesto, spinach, and ricotta cheese. Divide spinach mixture among mushroom caps. Bake, uncovered, in a 350° oven about 20 minutes or until mushrooms are tender and filling is heated through. Sprinkle with chopped tomatoes.

Nutrition Facts per serving: 260 cal., 19 g total fat (5 g sat. fat), 21 mg chol., 269 mg sodium, 11 g carbo., 5 g fiber, 11 g pro. Daily Values: 22% vit. A, 17% vit. C, 20% calcium, 8% iron

chapter 5

Salads

Big Green Salad with Two-Pepper Dressing

Strips of daikon add a pleasing crispness to fresh-tasting salad. Daikon is an Asian radish with a sweet taste and creamy white color. Look for it in the produce section of large supermarkets or Asian grocery stores.

Start to Finish: 30 minutes   Makes: 6 side-dish servings

- 1 recipe Two-Pepper Dressing
- 4 cups torn butterhead lettuce (2 medium heads)
- 1 cup fresh mint sprigs
- 1 cup fresh watercress sprigs
- ¾ cup fresh cilantro sprigs
- 1 cup daikon, peeled and cut into 1-inch strips

1 Prepare Two-Pepper Dressing; set aside. Rinse lettuce, mint, watercress, and cilantro in cold water; pat dry.

2 In a large bowl combine the rinsed and dried greens and daikon. Slowly add Two-Pepper Dressing; toss to coat. Serve immediately.

Two-Pepper Dressing: In a screw-top jar combine ½ cup finely chopped green sweet pepper; ⅓ cup rice vinegar; 3 tablespoons salad oil; 1 fresh Anaheim or jalapeño chile pepper, seeded and finely chopped*; and 1 clove garlic, minced. Add ½ teaspoon no-calorie heat-stable granular sugar substitute (Splenda), ¼ teaspoon salt, and ¼ teaspoon freshly ground black pepper. Cover; shake well. Refrigerate until ready to use.

∗Note: Because chile peppers, such as jalapeños, contain volatile oils that can burn your skin and eyes, wear plastic or rubber gloves when working with them. If your bare hands do touch the chile peppers, wash your hands well with soap and water.

Nutrition Facts per serving: 89 cal., 7 g total fat (1 g sat. fat), 0 mg chol., 114 mg sodium, 5 g carbo., 2 g fiber, 2 g pro.
Daily Values: 29% vit. A, 61% vit. C, 6% calcium, 17% iron

Mixed Greens with Raspberry Vinaigrette

Make the vinaigrette up to 2 days before serving and store in a covered jar in the refrigerator.

Start to Finish: 15 minutes Makes: 4 side-dish servings
- 6 cups torn mixed salad greens
- 2 tablespoons walnut oil or olive oil
- 2 tablespoons raspberry or red wine vinegar
- 2 teaspoons snipped fresh cilantro or parsley
- ½ cup chopped toasted walnuts
- Shaved or shredded Parmesan cheese (optional)

1 Place salad greens in a large salad bowl; set aside. For dressing, in a screw-top jar combine oil, vinegar, and cilantro. Cover and shake well; drizzle over greens. Sprinkle with walnuts. If desired, sprinkle with Parmesan cheese.

Nutrition Facts per serving: 170 cal., 17 g total fat (2 g sat. fat), 0 mg chol., 11 mg sodium, 4 g carbo., 2 g fiber, 3 g pro.
Daily Values: 16% vit. A, 9% vit. C, 5% calcium, 5% iron

2
net carbs

Sesame Spinach Salad

Seedless English cucumbers are preferred, but if you can't find them a regular cucumber will add the same crisp crunch and fresh flavor. Look for tahini salad dressing in health food stores.

Start to Finish: 10 minutes Makes: 4 side-dish servings

- 1 6-ounce package fresh baby spinach or one 8-ounce package torn mixed salad greens
- ½ cup thinly sliced English cucumber
- ¼ cup coarsely shredded red radish or daikon
- ½ cup bottled tahini salad dressing or oil and vinegar salad dressing
- 1 tablespoon toasted sesame seeds

1 In a large salad bowl combine spinach, cucumber, and radish. Pour dressing over salad; toss to coat. Sprinkle with sesame seeds.

Nutrition Facts per serving: 167 cal., 14 g total fat (1 g sat. fat), 0 mg chol., 392 mg sodium, 6 g carbo., 4 g fiber, 3 g pro.
Daily Values: 46% vit. A, 18% vit. C, 8% calcium, 19% iron

Asian Pea Pod Salad

4 net carbs

Start to Finish: 20 minutes Makes: 6 side-dish servings

- 6 cups torn romaine lettuce
- 2 cups fresh pea pods, trimmed and halved crosswise
- ⅓ cup bottled Italian salad dressing
- 1 tablespoon hoisin sauce
- 1 tablespoon toasted sesame seeds

1 In a large salad bowl toss together the lettuce and pea pods. In a small bowl stir together the salad dressing and hoisin sauce; pour over lettuce mixture. Toss to coat. Sprinkle with sesame seeds.

Nutrition Facts per serving: 98 cal., 7 g total fat (1 g sat. fat), 0 mg chol., 153 mg sodium, 6 g carbo., 2 g fiber, 2 g pro.
Daily Values: 31% vit. A, 25% vit. C, 4% calcium, 6% iron

3 net carbs

Mozzarella Caprese

Start to Finish: 10 minutes Makes: 8 side-dish servings
- 4 medium or 6 roma tomatoes
- 4 ounces fresh mozzarella balls
- 2 tablespoons bottled balsamic vinaigrette salad dressing
- ½ cup loosely packed fresh basil leaves, thinly sliced
- Salt and freshly ground black pepper

1 Cut tomatoes into ½-inch slices. Cut mozzarella into ¼-inch slices. Arrange tomato and cheese slices on a platter. Drizzle with vinaigrette. Sprinkle basil shreds on top. Sprinkle with salt and pepper to taste.

Nutrition Facts per serving: 64 cal., 4 g total fat (2 g sat. fat), 11 mg chol., 174 mg sodium, 4 g carbo., 1 g fiber, 3 g pro.
Daily Values: 12% vit. A, 20% vit. C, 8% calcium, 2% iron

Romaine with Creamy Garlic Dressing

You will have some of the salad dressing left over; cover and chill it up to 3 days.

Start to Finish: 5 minutes Makes: 4 side-dish servings
- ½ cup plain yogurt
- ⅓ cup bottled Italian salad dressing
- 1 clove garlic, minced
- 4 cups torn romaine
- ¼ cup finely shredded Parmesan cheese

1 For dressing, in a small bowl stir together yogurt, salad dressing, and garlic.

2 Arrange romaine on 4 salad plates. Drizzle each salad with 1 tablespoon of the dressing. Sprinkle salads with Parmesan cheese.

Nutrition Facts per serving: 257 cal., 19 g total fat (7 g sat. fat), 26 mg chol., 744 mg sodium, 7 g carbo., 1 g fiber, 15 g pro.
Daily Values: 34% vit. A, 23% vit. C, 50% calcium, 5% iron

Spinach Salad with Strawberries

Many bottled salad dressings contain sugar or corn syrup, two ingredients that boost carb totals. Check the ingredients list to be sure you buy one that is sugar-free and compare brands to find one low in carbohydrates.

Start to Finish: 20 minutes Makes: 4 side-dish servings
- 4 cups torn fresh spinach
- 1 cup watercress leaves
- 1 cup sliced fresh strawberries
- ½ of a small red onion, thinly sliced
- ½ cup bottled oil and vinegar salad dressing

1 In a large salad bowl combine spinach, watercress, strawberries, and onion. Pour dressing over salad; toss to coat.

Nutrition Facts per serving: 168 cal., 16 g total fat (2 g sat. fat), 0 mg chol., 468 mg sodium, 8 g carbo., 2 g fiber, 2 g pro.
Daily Values: 41% vit. A, 68% vit. C, 11% iron

Creamy Lemon-Pepper Coleslaw

Although the carrot in the packaged coleslaw mix elevates the carb level slightly, this fresh convenience food is a helpful timesaver for the busy cook. If you wish to avoid carrots, substitute 5 cups shredded cabbage.

Prep: 10 minutes Chill: 2 to 24 hours Makes: 6 side-dish servings

- ½ cup mayonnaise
- 1 teaspoon lemon-pepper seasoning
- ½ teaspoon dried thyme, crushed
- 5 cups packaged shredded cabbage with carrot (coleslaw mix)
- ¼ cup shelled sunflower seeds

1 In a large salad bowl combine mayonnaise, lemon-pepper seasoning, and thyme. Stir in shredded cabbage and sunflower seeds. Toss lightly to coat. Cover and chill for 2 to 24 hours.

Nutrition Facts per serving: 188 cal., 18 g total fat (2 g sat. fat), 7 mg chol., 328 mg sodium, 5 g carbo., 2 g fiber, 2 g pro.
Daily Values: 59% vit. A, 30% vit. C, 3% calcium, 5% iron

Napa Cabbage Slaw

Start to Finish: 30 minutes   Makes: 6 side-dish servings

- 3   cups finely shredded napa cabbage
- 1   cup finely shredded bok choy
- 2   to 3 tablespoons very thin red sweet pepper strips
- ¼   cup seasoned rice vinegar or white vinegar
- 1   tablespoon toasted sesame oil

1 In a large salad bowl combine cabbage, bok choy, and sweet pepper strips. In a small bowl stir together vinegar and sesame oil; pour over salad mixture. Toss to coat.

Nutrition Facts per serving: 29 cal., 2 g total fat (0 g sat. fat), 0 mg chol., 5 mg sodium, 2 g carbo., 1 g fiber, 1 g pro.
Daily Values: 7% vit. A, 27% vit. C, 3% calcium, 1% iron

Ginger-Tomato Salad

4 net carbs

Prep: 15 minutes **Chill:** 1 hour **Makes:** 4 side-dish servings
- 2 tablespoons rice vinegar
- 1 tablespoon finely minced fresh ginger
- 1 tablespoon no-calorie heat-stable granular sugar substitute (Splenda)
- ⅛ teaspoon salt
- 2 cups cherry or grape tomatoes

1 For dressing, in a small bowl whisk together rice vinegar, ginger, sugar substitute, and salt. Add tomatoes; toss gently to coat. Cover and chill for 1 to 4 hours.

Nutrition Facts per serving: 25 cal., 0 g total fat, 0 mg chol., 82 mg sodium, 5 g carbo., 1 g fiber, 1 g pro.
Daily Values: 12% vit. A, 30% vit. C, 1% calcium, 6% iron

3
net carbs

Minted French Green Beans

Haricots vert (ah-ree-co VARE)—thin, sweet green beans—are available from April through July. Store haricots vert for several days in the refrigerator.

Prep: 15 minutes Chill: 2 hours Makes: 4 side-dish servings

  8 ounces haricots vert or other small, thin green beans (2 cups)
  1 tablespoon minced shallot
  2 teaspoons olive oil
  2 teaspoons snipped fresh mint
    Salt and black pepper

1 Rinse beans. If desired, trim tips off beans. Place a steamer basket in a large skillet. Add water to just below the bottom of basket.

2 Bring water to boiling; add beans to basket. Steam, covered, for 2 minutes. Drain. Rinse with cold water; drain well. (Or plunge beans into ice water; drain well.)

3 In a medium salad bowl toss beans with shallot, oil, and mint. Season to taste with salt and pepper. Cover and chill for 2 hours.

Nutrition Facts per serving: 40 cal., 2 g total fat (0 g sat. fat), 0 mg chol., 39 mg sodium, 5 g carbo., 2 g fiber, 1 g pro.
Daily Values: 4% vit. A, 14% vit. C, 2% calcium, 4% iron

Rosemary-Splashed Veggie Salad

Prep: 15 minutes Chill: 2 to 24 hours Makes: 8 side-dish servings
- 1 cup bottled oil and vinegar salad dressing
- 2 teaspoons snipped fresh rosemary or 1 teaspoon dried rosemary, crushed
- ¼ teaspoon dry mustard
- 6 cups assorted fresh vegetables (such as fresh green beans or pea pods, trimmed; broccoli or cauliflower florets; coarsely chopped sweet pepper; and/or sliced celery)

1 In a large salad bowl stir together salad dressing, rosemary, and dry mustard. Add vegetables; toss to coat. Cover and chill for 2 to 24 hours, stirring occasionally.

Nutrition Facts per serving: 162 cal., 16 g total fat (3 g sat. fat), 0 mg chol., 19 mg sodium, 5 g carbo., 3 g fiber, 2 g pro.
Daily Values: 11% vit. A, 81% vit. C, 3% calcium, 4% iron

Roasted Eggplant and Sweet Pepper Salad

Prep: 5 minutes Roast: 20 minutes Stand: 10 minutes Oven: 425°F
Makes: 4 side-dish servings

- 1   medium eggplant (about 1 pound)
- 1   large red sweet pepper
- 1   tablespoon olive oil
- ⅛   teaspoon salt
- ½   of an 8-ounce container plain yogurt
- 1   tablespoon toasted pine nuts

1 Trim and discard ends from eggplant; halve eggplant lengthwise. Pierce skin several times. Halve sweet pepper lengthwise; remove and discard stem, seeds, and membranes. Place eggplant and sweet pepper halves, cut sides down, on a lightly greased baking sheet. Brush vegetables with some of the olive oil.

2 Roast eggplant and sweet pepper halves in a 425° oven for 20 to 25 minutes or until skins char slightly and blister. Remove from oven. Wrap sweet pepper halves in foil; let stand for 10 to 15 minutes or until cool enough to handle.

3 Peel eggplant and sweet pepper halves. Cut into large pieces. Toss with remaining oil and salt. Drizzle each serving with yogurt; sprinkle with pine nuts.

Nutrition Facts per serving: 98 cal., 5 g total fat (1 g sat. fat), 1 mg chol., 99 mg sodium, 12 g carbo., 4 g fiber, 4 g pro.
Daily Values: 42% vit. A, 103% vit. C, 7% calcium, 4% iron

Curried Egg Salad

Ground curry is the secret to making this egg salad "eggstraordinary." Serve it on a lettuce leaf or as a wrap in a low-carb tortilla.

2
net carbs

Prep: 15 minutes Chill: 4 to 24 hours Makes: 4 main-dish servings
- 8 hard-cooked eggs, chopped (see note, page 122)
- ½ cup mayonnaise
- ¼ cup finely chopped pitted ripe olives
- 2 tablespoons finely chopped green onion (1)
- ½ to 1 teaspoon curry powder
- ¼ teaspoon salt

1 In a medium bowl combine chopped eggs, mayonnaise, olives, green onion, curry powder, and salt. Cover and chill for 4 to 24 hours.

Nutrition Facts per serving: 367 cal., 34 g total fat (6 g sat. fat), 434 mg chol., 493 mg sodium, 2 g carbo., 0 g fiber, 13 g pro.
Daily Values: 12% vit. A, 1% vit. C, 6% calcium, 9% iron

Hot Italian Beef Salad

Start to Finish: 20 minutes Makes: 4 main-dish servings
- 12 ounces beef flank steak or beef top round steak, cut 1 inch thick
- 6 cups packaged torn mixed salad greens
- 3 teaspoons olive oil or salad oil
- 1 medium red or green sweet pepper, cut into bite-size strips
- ½ cup bottled Italian salad dressing or red wine vinegar and oil salad dressing
  Coarsely ground black pepper

1 Trim fat from steak. Cut steak into thin, bite-size strips. Arrange salad greens on 4 salad plates; set aside.

2 In a large skillet heat 2 teaspoons of the oil; add sweet pepper to skillet. Cook and stir for 1 to 2 minutes or until nearly crisp-tender.

3 Add the remaining 1 teaspoon oil to the skillet; add steak strips. Cook and stir for 2 to 3 minutes or to desired doneness. Add salad dressing to skillet. Cook and stir until heated through.

4 Spoon beef mixture over salad greens. Sprinkle with pepper.

Nutrition Facts per serving: 317 cal., 24 g total fat (5 g sat. fat), 34 mg chol., 284 mg sodium, 7 g carbo., 2 g fiber, 20 g pro.
Daily Values: 40% vit. A, 100% vit. C, 3% calcium, 11% iron

Tomato, Beef, and Basil Salad

The tomatoes account for about half of the carbs in this salad. If you like, leave them out and reduce the carbohydrate count by 3 grams of net carbs per serving.

Prep: 15 minutes Broil: 12 minutes Makes: 4 main-dish servings

- 12 ounces boneless beef top loin steak, cut 1 inch thick
- ¼ teaspoon salt
- ¼ teaspoon black pepper
- ⅔ cup bottled oil and vinegar salad dressing
- 6 cups torn mixed salad greens
- 2 cups red and/or yellow cherry tomatoes, halved
- 1 cup fresh basil leaves, cut into long, thin strips

1 Preheat broiler. Sprinkle meat with salt and pepper; brush with 2 tablespoons of the salad dressing. Place meat on the unheated rack of a broiler pan. Broil 3 to 4 inches from the heat until desired doneness, turning once halfway through broiling. Allow 12 to 14 minutes for medium rare (145°F) or 15 to 18 minutes for medium (160°F).

2 Meanwhile, in a large bowl combine salad greens, tomatoes, and basil. Add remaining salad dressing; toss to coat. Arrange greens mixture on 4 salad plates. Thinly slice steak across the grain; arrange steak slices on greens mixture.

Nutrition Facts per serving: 326 cal., 25 g total fat (5 g sat. fat), 40 mg chol., 210 mg sodium, 8 g carbo., 2 g fiber, 20 g pro. Daily Values: 35% vit. A, 41% vit. C, 7% calcium, 17% iron

Dijon Pork Salad

Prep: 10 minutes Roast: 20 minutes Oven: 425°F Makes: 4 main-dish servings

- 1   1-pound pork tenderloin
     Salt and black pepper
- ⅔   cup bottled Dijon lime salad dressing or oil and vinegar salad dressing
- 8   cups torn mixed salad greens
- 2   ounces Gouda or white cheddar cheese, cut into bite-size strips
- 12   cherry tomatoes, quartered

1 Trim fat from pork. Place pork on a rack in a shallow roasting pan. Sprinkle with salt and pepper. Brush pork with 2 tablespoons of the salad dressing. Roast in a 425° oven for 20 to 30 minutes or until done (160°F).

2 Meanwhile, arrange salad greens on 4 salad plates. Top with cheese and tomatoes. Thinly slice pork; arrange pork slices on salads. Serve with remaining salad dressing.

Nutrition Facts per serving: 336 cal., 24 g total fat (5 g sat. fat), 71 mg chol., 535 mg sodium, 5 g carbo., 2 g fiber, 23 g pro.
Daily Values: 16% vit. A, 24% vit. C, 13% calcium, 10% iron

B.L.T. Salad

Savor the flavors of a bacon, lettuce, and tomato sandwich minus the bread. This quick-to-fix salad features the same trio of ingredients.

Start to Finish: 20 minutes Makes: 4 main-dish or 8 side-dish servings

- 5 cups torn mixed salad greens
- 2 cups grape tomatoes, halved
- 10 slices bacon, crisp-cooked, drained, and crumbled
- 2 hard-cooked eggs, chopped (see note, page 122)
- ⅓ cup bottled poppy seed salad dressing

1 In a large salad bowl toss together salad greens, tomatoes, bacon, and eggs. Drizzle with salad dressing. Toss to coat.

Nutrition Facts per main-dish serving: 251 cal., 20 g total fat (5 g sat. fat), 123 mg chol., 461 mg sodium, 8 g carbo., 2 g fiber, 10 g pro. Daily Values: 50% vit. A, 57% vit. C, 6% calcium, 10% iron

Warm Chicken and Wilted Greens

Start to Finish: 25 minutes Makes: 4 main-dish servings
- 2 cups frozen pepper stir-fry vegetables
- 1 9-ounce package frozen chopped, cooked chicken breast, thawed
- ¼ cup bottled sesame salad dressing
- 6 cups fresh baby spinach and/or torn leaf lettuce

1 In a 12-inch skillet prepare frozen stir-fry vegetables according to package directions. Stir in chicken and salad dressing; heat through. Add spinach. Toss mixture in skillet for 30 to 60 seconds or until spinach is just wilted.

Nutrition Facts per serving: 153 cal., 6 g total fat (1 g sat. fat), 34 mg chol., 309 mg sodium, 8 g carbo., 2 g fiber, 17 g pro.
Daily Values: 65% vit. A, 46% vit. C, 6% calcium, 8% iron

Orange-Chicken Salad

Prep: 20 minutes Chill: 2 to 4 hours Makes: 6 main-dish servings
- 2 large oranges
- 1 cup mayonnaise
- ¾ teaspoon lemon-pepper seasoning
- 5 cups cubed or shredded cooked chicken
- ½ cup chopped toasted pecans or walnuts

1 Finely shred 1 teaspoon peel from 1 of the oranges. Cut the orange in half; squeeze orange until you have 2 tablespoons juice. Peel and section the remaining orange; cut sections into bite-size pieces.

2 In a medium bowl combine orange peel, orange juice, mayonnaise, and lemon-pepper seasoning. Stir in orange sections, chicken, and nuts. Cover and chill for 2 to 4 hours.

Nutrition Facts per serving: 558 cal., 44 g total fat (7 g sat. fat), 117 mg chol., 436 mg sodium, 3 g carbo., 1 g fiber, 35 g pro.
Daily Values: 2% vit. A, 14% vit. C, 3% calcium, 9% iron

4 net carbs

Ranch-Style Chicken Salad

Start to Finish: 10 minutes Makes: 4 main-dish servings
- 1   10-ounce package torn mixed salad greens
- ½   cup bottled ranch salad dressing
- 1   6-ounce package refrigerated cooked chicken breast strips
- 1   cup sliced fresh mushrooms
- ½   cup shredded Monterey Jack cheese with jalapeño peppers (2 ounces)

1 In a large salad bowl toss together salad greens and dressing. Divide salad greens among 4 dinner plates. Arrange chicken strips and mushrooms on top of greens. Sprinkle each serving with cheese.

Nutrition Facts per serving: 280 cal., 23 g total fat (6 g sat. fat), 46 mg chol., 712 mg sodium, 5 g carbo., 1 g fiber, 16 g pro.
Daily Values: 22% vit. A, 10% vit. C, 14% calcium, 4% iron

Chicken Salad with Olives and Peppers

Soft cream cheese with chives and onion serves as the dressing in this savory chicken salad. Roasted red pepper and green olives add sparks of color.

Prep: 15 minutes Chill: 2 to 24 hours Makes: 4 main-dish servings

- 2 cups chopped cooked chicken
- ¼ cup chopped toasted walnuts
- ¼ cup chopped roasted red sweet peppers
- ¼ cup sliced pimiento-stuffed green olives
- ½ of an 8-ounce tub cream cheese with chives and onion
  Black pepper

1 In a medium bowl combine chicken, walnuts, sweet peppers, and olives. Add cream cheese, stirring until combined. Season to taste with black pepper. Cover and chill for 2 to 24 hours.

Nutrition Facts per serving: 229 cal., 16 g total fat (7 g sat. fat), 61 mg chol., 501 mg sodium, 4 g carbo., 1 g fiber, 17 g pro.
Daily Values: 9% vit. A, 45% vit. C, 5% calcium, 3% iron

2
net carbs

Turkey-Zucchini Salad

Prep: 20 minutes Chill: 4 to 24 hours Makes: 6 to 8 main-dish servings

- 3 cups finely chopped cooked turkey
- 2 stalks celery, chopped
- 1 medium zucchini or yellow summer squash, chopped
- 4 green onions, sliced
- 2 tablespoons finely chopped green sweet pepper
- 1 tablespoon lemon juice
- ⅛ teaspoon black pepper
- ⅔ cup mayonnaise
- 4 teaspoons Dijon-style mustard
  Lettuce leaves

1 In a large bowl combine turkey, celery, zucchini, green onions, sweet pepper, lemon juice, and black pepper. Stir in mayonnaise and mustard. Cover and chill for 4 to 24 hours before serving.

2 To serve, line each salad plate with lettuce leaves. Top each with turkey mixture.

Nutrition Facts per serving: 347 cal., 27 g total fat (5 g sat. fat), 86 mg chol., 290 mg sodium, 3 g carbo., 1 g fiber, 22 g pro.
Daily Values: 10% vit. A, 18% vit. C, 13% iron

Tarragon Tuna Salad

Start to Finish: 15 minutes Makes: 4 main-dish servings
- 1 10-ounce package torn mixed salad greens
- 1 cup chopped tomato
- 1 6½-ounce can chunk white tuna (water pack), drained and broken into chunks
- ⅓ cup bottled Caesar salad dressing
- 2 teaspoons snipped fresh tarragon or ¼ teaspoon dried tarragon, crushed

1 Arrange salad greens on 4 dinner plates. Top each salad with tomato and tuna. In a small bowl combine salad dressing and tarragon; drizzle over each salad.

Nutrition Facts per serving: 182 cal., 13 g total fat (2 g sat. fat), 20 mg chol., 398 mg sodium, 4 g carbo., 2 g fiber, 12 g pro. Daily Values: 11% vit. A, 19% vit. C, 3% calcium, 6% iron

4
net carbs

Tossed Shrimp Salad

This refreshing salad gets you in and out of the kitchen fast, allowing plenty of time for after-dinner exercise such as a bike ride or long walk.

Start to Finish: 10 minutes Makes: 4 main-dish servings

- 2 8-ounce packages frozen peeled, cooked shrimp, thawed
- 1 10-ounce package torn mixed salad greens
- ¼ cup thinly sliced green onions (2)
- ⅓ cup bottled Italian salad dressing
   Salt and black pepper (optional)
- ¼ cup sliced toasted almonds

1 Rinse and drain shrimp; pat dry with paper towels.

2 In a large salad bowl combine shrimp, salad greens, and green onions. Pour dressing over salad; toss to coat. If desired, season to taste with salt and pepper. Sprinkle with almonds.

Nutrition Facts per serving: 301 cal., 20 g total fat (2 g sat. fat), 185 mg chol., 483 mg sodium, 6 g carbo., 2 g fiber, 26 g pro.
Daily Values: 9% vit. A, 10% vit. C, 10% calcium, 20% iron

Vegetables and Side Dishes

2 net carbs

Vegetables with Tarragon Butter

Start to Finish: 20 minutes Makes: 10 servings
- 1 tablespoon snipped fresh tarragon or ¼ teaspoon dried tarragon, crushed
- 1 tablespoon dry white wine (optional)
- ½ cup butter, softened
- 5 to 6 cups steamed green beans, asparagus, sliced zucchini, and/or sliced yellow summer squash

1 Stir tarragon and, if desired, wine into softened butter. Toss butter mixture with hot cooked vegetables.

Nutrition Facts per serving: 103 cal., 10 g total fat (6 g sat. fat), 26 mg chol., 102 mg sodium, 4 g carbo., 2 g fiber, 1 g pro.
Daily Values: 14% vit. A, 13% vit. C, 2% calcium, 3% iron

Asparagus and Fresh Mozzarella

Look for lemon verbena, an herb that has a strong lemon flavor, in the produce section of supermarkets or farmers' markets. If you can't find it, use lemon peel. It imparts the same piquant flavor.

Start to Finish: 15 minutes Makes: 4 to 6 servings
- 1 pound asparagus spears
- 2 ounces fresh mozzarella cheese, cut or torn into pieces
- 1 teaspoon snipped fresh lemon verbena or ¼ teaspoon finely shredded lemon peel

1 Snap off and discard woody bases from asparagus. Using a sharp knife, carefully split asparagus stalks lengthwise.

2 Place a steamer basket in a large skillet. Add water to just below the bottom of the steamer basket. Bring water to boiling. Add asparagus to steamer basket. Cover and steam for 1 minute. Transfer asparagus to a broiler-proof serving dish; top with mozzarella cheese.

3 Broil asparagus 4 inches from heat about 2 minutes or until cheese bubbles slightly. Just before serving, sprinkle with lemon verbena.

Nutrition Facts per serving: 56 cal., 3 g total fat (2 g sat. fat), 11 mg chol., 134 mg sodium, 2 g carbo., 1 g fiber, 5 g pro.
Daily Values: 4% vit. A, 26% vit. C, 8% calcium, 3% iron

Asparagus in Mustard-Dill Sauce

If dill mustard is not available, substitute 2 tablespoons Dijon-style mustard plus 1 teaspoon snipped fresh dill.

Prep: 10 minutes Bake: 15 minutes Oven: 425°F Makes: 4 servings
- 2 pounds fresh asparagus spears
- ¼ cup reduced-sodium chicken broth
- 2 tablespoons dill mustard
- Coarsely ground black pepper
- 2 tablespoons grated Parmesan or Asiago cheese (optional)

1 Snap off and discard woody bases from asparagus. Arrange asparagus in a shallow baking dish. Combine chicken broth and mustard; pour over asparagus, turning to coat.

2 Bake, uncovered, in a 425° oven for 15 to 20 minutes or until asparagus is crisp-tender. Transfer to a serving dish; sprinkle with pepper. If desired, sprinkle with cheese.

Nutrition Facts per serving: 4 cal., 2 g total fat (1 g sat. fat), 2 mg chol., 290 mg sodium, 4 g carbo., 2 g fiber, 4 g pro.
Daily Values: 13% vit. A, 23% vit. C, 4% calcium, 4% iron

Roasted Asparagus Parmesan

Prep: 10 minutes Bake: 15 minutes Oven: 400°F Makes: 6 servings

- 2 pounds fresh asparagus spears
- 2 tablespoons olive oil
- Salt and black pepper
- ½ cup finely grated Parmesan cheese

1 Snap off and discard woody bases from asparagus spears. If desired, scrape off scales. Place asparagus in a 15×10×1-inch baking pan. Drizzle with olive oil, tossing gently to coat. Spread out into a single layer. Sprinkle with salt and pepper.

2 Bake in a 400° oven about 15 minutes or until asparagus is crisp-tender. Transfer asparagus to a serving platter; sprinkle with Parmesan cheese.

Nutrition Facts per serving: 95 cal., 7 g total fat (2 g sat. fat), 8 mg chol., 102 mg sodium, 4 g carbo., 2 g fiber, 5 g pro.
Daily Values: 5% vit. A, 94% vit. C, 6% calcium, 4% iron

Oven-Roasted Broccoli

Prep: 5 minutes Roast: 20 minutes Oven: 450°F Makes: 4 to 6 servings

- 2   tablespoons olive oil
- 4   cups broccoli florets
- 1   cup thinly sliced leek
- ½ teaspoon salt
- ¼ teaspoon black pepper

1 Add oil to a shallow baking pan. Heat in a 450° oven for 1 minute. Stir broccoli into hot oil. Bake, covered, for 15 minutes.

2 Stir leek, salt, and pepper into baking pan. Roast, covered, for 5 to 7 minutes more or until broccoli is crisp-tender.

Nutrition Facts per serving: 98 cal., 7 g total fat (1 g sat. fat), 0 mg chol., 319 mg sodium, 8 g carbo., 3 g fiber, 3 g pro.
Daily Values: 26% vit. A, 121% vit. C, 6% calcium, 7% iron.

Lemon Broccoli

This broccoli side dish with olive oil, lemon, and garlic pairs beautifully with roast pork tenderloin.

Start to Finish: 25 minutes Makes: 4 servings
- 4 cups broccoli florets
- 1 tablespoon olive oil
- ½ teaspoon finely shredded lemon peel
- ¼ teaspoon salt
- ¼ teaspoon black pepper
- 1 clove garlic, minced
  Lemon wedges (optional)

1 Place a steamer basket in a large saucepan. Add water to just below the bottom of the steamer basket. Bring water to boiling. Add broccoli to steamer basket. Cover and steam over high heat for 5 to 6 minutes or just until broccoli is tender.

2 Meanwhile, in a large serving bowl combine olive oil, lemon peel, salt, pepper, and garlic. Add broccoli; toss to coat. If desired, garnish with lemon wedges.

Nutrition Facts per serving: 56 cal., 4 g total fat (1 g sat. fat), 0 mg chol., 169 mg sodium, 5 g carbo., 3 g fiber, 3 g pro.
Daily Values: 27% vit. A, 138% vit. C, 4% calcium, 5% iron

3
net carbs

Brussels Sprouts with Prosciutto

When buying fresh Brussels sprouts look for firm, compact heads. The larger, older Brussels sprouts are bitter. The smaller, vivid green ones are the sweetest.

Start to Finish: 25 minutes Makes: 12 servings

- 1½ pounds Brussels sprouts
- 3 ounces prosciutto, chopped
- 1 teaspoon finely shredded lemon peel
- ½ teaspoon salt
- ¼ teaspoon black pepper

1 Trim stems and remove any wilted outer leaves from Brussels sprouts; rinse with cold water. Cook, covered, in enough boiling salted water to cover for 10 to 12 minutes or until crisp-tender. Drain; rinse with cold water. Thinly slice Brussels sprouts.

2 Heat a 12-inch nonstick skillet 1 minute over medium-high heat. Add Brussels sprouts. Cook and stir for 2 to 3 minutes or until heated through. Stir in prosciutto, lemon peel, salt, and pepper.

Nutrition Facts per : 36 cal., 1 g total fat (0 g sat. fat), 5 mg chol., 301 mg sodium, 5 g carbo., 2 g fiber, 4 g pro.
Daily Values: 9% vit. A, 62% vit. C, 2% calcium, 4% iron

Curried Cauliflower

Prep: 5 minutes Cook: 8 minutes Makes: 4 servings
- 4 cups cauliflower florets
- 2 tablespoons butter
- 2 tablespoons sliced green onion (1)
- 1 teaspoon curry powder
- ⅛ teaspoon crushed red pepper
- Salt

1 In a medium saucepan cook cauliflower, covered, in a small amount of boiling salted water for 8 to 10 minutes or just until crisp-tender. Drain; set aside.

2 Melt butter in the same saucepan over medium heat. Add green onion; cook and stir for 30 seconds. Stir in curry powder and crushed red pepper. Stir in cauliflower. Season to taste with salt.

Nutrition Facts per serving: 82 cal., 6 g total fat (4 g sat. fat), 16 mg chol., 128 mg sodium, 6 g carbo., 3 g fiber, 2 g pro. Daily Values: 5% vit. A, 67% vit. C, 3% calcium, 4% iron

5
net carbs

Roasted Fennel and Onions

Prep: 15 minutes **Roast:** 35 minutes **Oven:** 400°F **Makes:** 6 servings

- 2 medium fennel bulbs
- 1 large onion, cut into 1-inch wedges
- 2 tablespoons olive oil
- ½ teaspoon fennel seeds or dried Italian seasoning, crushed
- ½ teaspoon salt
- ¼ teaspoon black pepper

1 To prepare fennel, cut off and discard upper stalks. Remove any wilted outer layers and cut a thin slice from the fennel base. Wash fennel and cut in half lengthwise. Cut lengthwise into wedges about 1 inch thick. Place fennel and onion in a shallow roasting pan. Drizzle with olive oil; sprinkle with fennel seeds, salt, and pepper. Stir to coat.

2 Roast in a 400° oven for 35 to 40 minutes or until vegetables are light brown and tender, stirring twice.

Nutrition Facts per serving: 75 cal., 5 g total fat (1 g sat. fat), 0 mg chol., 235 mg sodium, 8 g carbo., 3 g fiber, 1 g pro.
Daily Values: 2% vit. A, 19% vit. C, 5% calcium, 4% iron

Green Beans in Shallot Butter

Start to Finish: 25 minutes Makes: 8 servings
- 1½ pounds green beans
- 2 tablespoons butter
- ¼ cup minced shallots
- ½ teaspoon salt
- ¼ teaspoon black pepper

1 Place a steamer basket in a large saucepan. Add water to just below the bottom of the steamer basket. Bring water to boiling. Add beans to steamer basket. Cover and steam for 5 to 7 minutes or until crisp-tender.

2 Meanwhile, melt butter in a large skillet over medium-high heat; add shallots. Cook and stir for 1 minute. Add beans, salt, and pepper to skillet. Cook for 1 to 2 minutes more or until heated through.

Nutrition Facts per serving : 54 cal., 3 g total fat (2 g sat. fat), 8 mg chol., 181 mg sodium, 6 g carbo., 3 g fiber, 2 g pro.
Daily Values: 13% vit. A, 18% vit. C, 3% calcium, 5% iron

3
net carbs

Garlicky Green Beans

Simply prepared garden-fresh green beans are always a favorite. Cook them just until crisp-tender so they're still vibrantly green.

Start to Finish: 30 minutes Makes: 6 servings
- 1 pound green beans
- 2 tablespoons butter
- ½ teaspoon black pepper
- 2 cloves garlic, minced

1 In a Dutch oven or large saucepan cook green beans, covered, in a small amount of boiling salted water for 10 to 15 minutes or until crisp-tender. Drain; set beans aside.

2 Melt butter in the same pan over medium heat. Add pepper and garlic; cook and stir for 1 minute. Stir in green beans.

Nutrition Facts per serving: 61 cal., 4 g total fat (3 g sat. fat), 11 mg chol., 143 mg sodium, 6 g carbo., 3 g fiber, 2 g pro.
Daily Values: 12% vit. A, 16% vit. C, 3% calcium, 5% iron

Green Beans and Bacon

Bacon gives an old-fashioned flavor to a package of frozen green beans.

Start to Finish: 30 minutes Makes: 6 servings
- 4 slices bacon
- 1 9-ounce package frozen whole green beans, thawed
- 3 medium carrots, cut into julienne strips
- 1 tablespoon butter
- 1 clove garlic, minced
- ¼ teaspoon black pepper

1 In a large skillet cook bacon over medium heat until crisp. Remove bacon, reserving 2 tablespoons drippings in skillet; drain bacon on paper towels. Crumble bacon; set aside.

2 Add green beans, carrots, butter, and garlic to reserved drippings in skillet. Cook and stir over medium-high heat about 5 minutes or until vegetables are crisp-tender. Stir in pepper. Transfer vegetable mixture to a serving bowl; sprinkle with bacon.

Nutrition Facts per serving: 187 cal., 17 g total fat (7 g sat. fat), 22 mg chol., 218 mg sodium, 7 g carbo., 2 g fiber, 3 g pro.
Daily Values: 177% vit. A, 12% vit. C, 3% calcium, 4% iron

5
net carbs

Green Beans and Fennel

Chopped, fresh fennel offers the delightful crunch of celery, but with a subtle licorice flavor. To crush fennel seeds, place them on a cutting board, then roll over them with a rolling pin.

Start to Finish: 30 minutes Makes: 10 to 12 servings

- 2 tablespoons butter, softened
- 1½ teaspoons fennel seeds, crushed
- 1½ teaspoons finely shredded lemon peel
- ¾ teaspoon black pepper
- ¼ teaspoon salt
- 3 fennel bulbs (3 pounds)
- 1¾ pounds fresh green beans, trimmed if desired

1 In a large bowl stir together butter, fennel seeds, lemon peel, pepper, and salt; set aside.

2 Cut off and discard upper stalks of fennel bulbs. Remove any wilted outer layers; cut off a thin slice from the fennel base. Wash fennel; cut into quarters. Remove cores. Cut fennel lengthwise into ¼-inch strips.

3 Place beans in a 4-quart Dutch oven. Cook beans, covered, in a small amount of boiling salted water 4 to 5 minutes. Add fennel strips to beans. Cook 6 to 10 minutes more or until vegetables are crisp-tender. Drain. Toss fennel and beans in the bowl with the seasoned butter. Transfer to a serving dish.

Nutrition Facts per serving: 67 cal., 3 g total fat (2 g sat. fat), 7 mg chol., 124 mg sodium, 10 g carbo., 5 g fiber, 2 g pro.
Daily Values: 12% vit. A, 29% vit. C, 6% calcium, 7% iron

Sautéed Broccoli Rabe

Broccoli rabe, also known as rapini, has a leafy green stalk with small clusters of broccoli-like florets. Find it at many supermarkets and specialty foods stores.

Start to Finish: 20 minutes Makes: 6 servings
- 2   pounds broccoli rabe or 6 cups coarsely chopped broccoli florets
- 3   cloves garlic, minced
- ¼   teaspoon salt
- 4   teaspoons olive oil
  Crushed red pepper (optional)

1 Wash broccoli rabe; remove and discard woody stems. Cut into 2-inch pieces. In a 12-inch skillet cook and stir broccoli rabe, garlic, and salt in hot oil over medium-high heat for 3 to 4 minutes or until broccoli rabe is crisp-tender. (If using broccoli florets, cook and stir for 5 to 6 minutes or until crisp-tender). If desired, sprinkle with crushed red pepper.

Nutrition Facts per serving: 71 cal., 4 g total fat (0 g sat. fat), 0 mg chol., 128 mg sodium, 8 g carbo., 5 g fiber, 5 g pro.
Daily Values: 188% vit. C, 6% calcium, 8% iron

3 net carbs

Swiss Chard with Peppered Bacon

Low in carbohydrates but rich in vitamins A and C, Swiss chard pairs nicely with roasted and grilled meats. Look for this leafy green vegetable in the summer months when it's at its peak.

Start to Finish: 20 minutes Makes: 4 servings

- 2 slices thick-sliced peppered bacon
- ½ cup chopped onion
- 8 cups coarsely chopped fresh Swiss chard leaves
- ½ teaspoon finely shredded lemon peel
  Salt and black pepper

1 In a 12-inch skillet cook bacon over medium heat until crisp. Remove bacon from skillet, reserving 1 tablespoon drippings in skillet; drain bacon on paper towels. Crumble bacon; set aside.

2 Cook onion in reserved drippings over medium heat until tender. Add Swiss chard. Cook and stir about 5 minutes or just until tender. Stir in bacon and lemon peel. Season to taste with salt and pepper.

Nutrition Facts per serving: 45 cal., 2 g total fat (1 g sat. fat), 3 mg chol., 253 mg sodium, 5 g carbo., 2 g fiber, 3 g pro.
Daily Values: 48% vit. A, 38% vit. C, 4% calcium, 8% iron

Beet Greens with Walnuts and Blue Cheese

Prep: 10 minutes Cook: 3 minutes Makes: 4 servings
- 8 ounces beet greens, fresh spinach, or Swiss chard
- 2 teaspoons cooking oil
- 2 tablespoons chopped walnuts
- 1 tablespoon crumbled blue cheese
- ¼ teaspoon coarsely ground black pepper

1 Wash greens thoroughly in cold water; drain well. Remove and discard stems. Cut greens into 1-inch strips; set aside.

2 In a large skillet heat oil over medium-high heat. Add walnuts; cook and stir for 2 minutes. Add greens; cook and stir about 1 minute or just until wilted. Remove from heat. Sprinkle with blue cheese and pepper.

Nutrition Facts per serving: 55 cal., 5 g total fat (1 g sat. fat), 0 mg chol., 109 mg sodium, 3 g carbo., 2 g fiber, 2 g pro.
Daily Values: 66% vit. A, 17% vit. C, 7% calcium, 10% iron

6
net carbs

Steamed Red Chard

Start to Finish: 45 minutes Makes: 6 servings
- 3 pounds red Swiss chard, stems removed and leaves cut crosswise into ½-inch strips
- 1 cup chopped onion
- 2 tablespoons olive oil
- ¼ cup sherry vinegar or red wine vinegar
- ½ teaspoon salt
- ½ teaspoon freshly ground black pepper

1 Fill a 4-quart Dutch oven with water to a depth of 1 inch. Bring water to boiling. Place a steamer basket in the Dutch oven. Place one-third of the chard in the steamer basket. Cover and steam 5 minutes or until chard is tender. Remove wilted chard from steamer basket and place in a large colander placed over a large bowl to drain; set aside. Repeat with remaining chard. Discard any water remaining in Dutch oven.

2 In the same Dutch oven cook onion in hot oil over medium heat until tender but not brown. Add steamed chard, vinegar, salt, and pepper. Cook and stir until heated through.

Nutrition Facts per serving: 94 cal., 5 g total fat (1 g sat. fat), 0 mg chol., 617 mg sodium, 10 g carbo., 4 g fiber, 4 g pro.
Daily Values: 131% vit. A, 65% vit. C, 11% calcium, 21% iron

Sautéed Spinach and Olives

Start to Finish: 10 minutes Makes: 2 servings
- 8 cups fresh spinach and/or mustard greens, stems removed
- 2 teaspoons olive oil
- ¼ cup pitted kalamata olives
- 1 ounce feta cheese

1 Wash spinach thoroughly in cold water; drain well. In a very large skillet heat olive oil over medium-high heat. Add olives; cook for 3 to 5 minutes, stirring once. Remove skillet from heat; toss spinach in hot oil with the hot olives.

2 Cut feta cheese into wedges (cheese will crumble slightly). Arrange cheese on a serving platter. Spoon greens and olives around cheese.

Nutrition Facts per serving: 116 cal., 10 g total fat (3 g sat. fat), 12 mg chol., 488 mg sodium, 2 g carbo., 12 g fiber, 6 g pro.
Daily Values: 130% vit. A, 30% vit. C, 16% calcium, 46% iron

3
net carbs

Herbed Mushrooms

Start to Finish: 25 minutes Makes: 6 to 8 servings

- 3 cloves garlic, minced
- 3 shallots, peeled and cut into thin wedges
- 2 tablespoons olive oil
- 8 cups sliced fresh button mushrooms
- ¼ cup snipped fresh tarragon, rosemary, basil, oregano, or parsley
- ¼ teaspoon salt
- ¼ teaspoon coarsely ground black pepper

1 In a large skillet cook garlic and shallots in hot oil over medium-high heat for 2 minutes. Add mushrooms to skillet. Cook, stirring occasionally, for 6 to 8 minutes or until tender. Stir in tarragon, salt, and pepper.

Nutrition Facts per serving: 81 cal., 5 g total fat (1 g sat. fat), 0 mg chol., 118 mg sodium, 5 g carbo., 2 g fiber, 5 g pro.
Daily Values: 3% vit. A, 2% vit. C, 1% calcium, 5% iron

Pea Pods and Onions with Dill Butter

Start to Finish: 15 minutes Makes: 10 to 12 servings

- 1 16-ounce package frozen small whole onions
- 2 6-ounce packages frozen pea pods
- 2 cloves garlic, minced, or 1 teaspoon bottled minced garlic
- 3 tablespoons butter
- 1 tablespoon snipped fresh dill or 1 teaspoon dried dill
- ½ teaspoon salt
- ¼ teaspoon white pepper
   Fresh dill sprigs (optional)

1 Cook onions in a small amount of boiling water in a large saucepan for 2 minutes. Add pea pods and cook 2 to 3 minutes more or just until tender, stirring occasionally. Drain.

2 Meanwhile, cook garlic in hot butter in a small saucepan for 30 seconds. Stir in dill, salt, and white pepper. Drizzle over vegetables, tossing to coat. If desired, garnish with fresh dill sprigs.

Nutrition Facts per serving: 64 cal., 4 g total fat (2 g sat. fat), 9 mg chol., 144 mg sodium, 7 g carbo., 2 g fiber, 2 g pro.
Daily Values: 3% vit. A, 14% vit. C, 2% calcium, 5% iron

5
net carbs

Teeny Zucchini with Onions

Three main ingredients and less than 10 minutes in the skillet reward you with a side dish that's sensational.

Prep: 10 minutes Cook: 7 minutes Makes: 4 to 6 servings
- 1 pound baby zucchini or 3 medium zucchini, halved lengthwise and cut into ½-inch slices
- 1 tablespoon olive oil
- 1 small onion, cut into thin wedges
- ¼ cup chopped walnuts
- ½ teaspoon dried oregano, crushed
- ¼ teaspoon salt
- ¼ teaspoon black pepper

1 Rinse and trim baby zucchini. Heat oil in a large nonstick skillet over medium heat. Add zucchini and onions. Cook, stirring occasionally, for 6 to 8 minutes or just until vegetables are tender. Add walnuts, oregano, salt, and pepper to skillet. Cook and stir for 1 minute more.

Nutrition Facts per serving: 106 cal., 9 g total fat (1 g sat. fat), 0 mg chol., 146 mg sodium, 6 g carbo., 1 g fiber, 4 g pro.
Daily Values: 67% vit. C, 3% calcium, 2% iron

Zucchini alla Romana

For best results, select zucchini that are small, firm, and free of cuts and soft spots. Pass over large zucchini, which tend to have tough skins and lots of seeds.

Prep: 8 minutes   Cook: 5 minutes   Makes: 6 servings
- 2   cloves garlic
- 2   teaspoons olive oil
- 4   cups sliced zucchini
- ¼   teaspoon salt
   Dash black pepper
- 2   tablespoons finely shredded Romano or Parmesan cheese
- 1   tablespoon snipped fresh mint or basil

1 In a large skillet cook whole garlic cloves in hot oil until light brown; discard garlic. Add zucchini, salt, and pepper to skillet. Cook over medium heat, stirring occasionally, about 5 minutes or until zucchini is crisp-tender. Sprinkle with Parmesan cheese and mint.

Nutrition Facts per serving: 35 cal., 2 g total fat (1 g sat. fat), 2 mg chol., 124 mg sodium, 3 g carbo., 1 g fiber, 2 g pro.
Daily Values: 5% vit. A, 11% vit. C, 4% calcium, 3% iron

Spiced Pumpkin Soup

Start to Finish: 15 minutes Makes: 6 servings

- 1 15-ounce can pumpkin
- 1 14-ounce can chicken broth
- 1 cup half-and-half, light cream, or milk
- 1 tablespoon no-calorie heat-stable granular sugar substitute (Splenda)
- ½ teaspoon pumpkin pie spice

1 In a medium saucepan stir together pumpkin, chicken broth, and half-and-half. Stir in sugar substitute and pumpkin pie spice. Heat through.

Nutrition Facts per serving: 86 cal., 5 g total fat (3 g sat. fat), 15 mg chol., 296 mg sodium, 8 g carbo., 2 g fiber, 3 g pro.
Daily Values: 317% vit. A, 6% vit. C, 7% calcium, 6% iron

chapter 7

Appetizers and Snacks

net carbs

Sausage-Stuffed Zucchini

Spicy sausage adds a touch of heat to this simple recipe. You can prepare the zucchini for roasting a day ahead for quicker assembly right before serving.

Prep: 15 minutes Roast: 20 minutes Oven: 450°F Makes: 24 rounds

- 2 medium zucchini
- 1 tablespoon olive oil
- ¼ teaspoon salt
- ⅛ teaspoon black pepper
- 8 ounces hot sausage, casings removed
- 2 teaspoons olive oil

1 Cut the ends from each zucchini and discard. Cut zucchini into ½-inch slices. With a small melon baller or measuring spoon, carefully scoop out about ¼ teaspoon of zucchini from center of each slice. Place zucchini slices in a roasting pan. Drizzle with the 1 tablespoon olive oil and sprinkle with salt and pepper. Toss to coat; arrange zucchini flat side down. Roast in a 450° oven for 20 to 25 minutes or until light brown and crisp-tender.

2 Meanwhile, in a large skillet cook sausage in hot olive oil over medium-high heat until no longer pink. Remove from heat. Spoon sausage into center of each zucchini round. Serve warm. Makes about 24 appetizers.

Nutrition Facts per appetizer: 43 cal., 4 g total fat (1 g sat. fat), 5 mg chol., 72 mg sodium, 1 g carbo., 0 g fiber, 1 g pro. Daily Values: 1% vit. A, 2% vit. C, 1% iron.

Prosciutto-Arugula Roll-Ups

For best results, purchase prosciutto that's thin enough to roll up easily but not so thin that it tears when you separate the slices. Ask your butcher to cut 8 slices that measure 9×3 inches and about 1/16 inch thick.

0
net carbs

Start to Finish: 30 minutes   Makes: about 48 slices
- 1 5-ounce container semisoft cheese with garlic and herb
- 2 ounces soft goat cheese (chèvre)
- ⅓ cup toasted pine nuts or chopped toasted almonds
- 4 ounces thinly sliced prosciutto (8 slices)
- 1½ cups arugula or spinach leaves, stems removed (about 2½ ounces)

1 In a medium bowl stir together the garlic and herb cheese, the goat cheese, and pine nuts. Spread about 2 tablespoons of the cheese mixture over each prosciutto slice. Top with arugula leaves. Roll up each slice from a short side. Cut into ½-inch slices. Serve immediately or cover and chill up to 6 hours.

Nutrition Facts per slice: 33 cal., 3 g total fat (1 g sat. fat), 4 mg chol., 55 mg sodium, 0 g carbo., 0 g fiber, 2 g pro.
Daily Values: 1% calcium, 1% iron

Chicken Skewers with Spicy Peanut Sauce

Can't take the heat? Stir the smaller amount of chile-garlic sauce into the peanut sauce.

Prep: 30 minutes Bake: 8 minutes Oven: 400°F Makes: 12 appetizers

- 12 6-inch wooden skewers
- ½ cup natural peanut butter
- 3 tablespoons rice vinegar
- 3 tablespoons reduced-sodium soy sauce
- 3 to 4 tablespoons water
- 2 to 3 teaspoons Oriental chile-garlic sauce
- 1 pound skinless, boneless chicken breast halves
   Lime wedges (optional)

1 Soak skewers in water for 30 minutes.

2 Meanwhile, for sauce, in a small saucepan combine peanut butter, vinegar, and soy sauce. Whisk over medium-low heat until peanut butter is melted and mixture is smooth. Whisk in water to reach desired consistency. Whisk in desired amount of chile-garlic sauce. Set aside.

3 Cut chicken into 12 long strips; thread accordion-style onto skewers. Arrange chicken skewers in a single layer on a lightly greased baking sheet. Bake in a 400° oven for 6 minutes. Brush with ¼ cup of the sauce. Bake 2 to 4 minutes more or until chicken is tender and no longer pink.

4 To serve, place chicken skewers on a serving platter. Whisk remaining sauce; pour into a serving bowl. Serve chicken skewers with sauce and, if desired, lime wedges.

Nutrition Facts per appetizer: 111 cal., 6 g total fat (1 g sat. fat), 22 mg chol., 220 mg sodium, 2 g carbo., 1 g fiber, 12 g pro.
Daily Values: 1% vit. C, 1% calcium, 3% iron

0
net carbs

Five-Spice Drummies

You can easily double the recipe, but with so many wings to bake you'll have to cook them in two batches so they brown evenly.

Prep: 5 minutes Marinate: 4 to 24 hours Bake: 30 minutes Oven: 400°F
Makes: 12 servings

- 24 fresh or frozen chicken wing drummettes (about 3 pounds)
- ¼ cup soy sauce
- ¼ cup orange juice
- 1 tablespoon no-calorie heat-stable granular sugar substitute (Splenda)
- 2 teaspoons five-spice powder

1 Thaw chicken wings, if frozen. Place chicken in a self-sealing plastic bag set in a large bowl. For marinade, in a small bowl stir together the soy sauce, orange juice, sugar substitute, and five-spice powder. Pour over chicken in bag; seal bag. Marinate in refrigerator for 4 to 24 hours.

2 Drain chicken, discarding marinade. Arrange chicken in a single layer in a 15×10×1-inch baking pan. Bake, uncovered, in a 400° oven for 30 to 35 minutes or until chicken is tender and no longer pink.

Nutrition Facts per serving: 247 cal., 18 g total fat (4 g sat. fat), 116 mg chol., 255 mg sodium, 0 g carbo., 0 g fiber, 20 g pro.
Daily Values: 0% vit. A, 2% vit. C, 1% iron

Buffalo Wings

Prep: 10 minutes Stand: 30 minutes Broil: 20 minutes Makes: 12 servings

12 chicken wings (about 2 pounds), with tips cut off
 2 tablespoons butter, melted
 2 to 3 tablespoons bottled hot pepper sauce
 1 teaspoon paprika
    Bottled blue cheese salad dressing

1 Cut wings at joints to form 24 pieces. Place chicken pieces in a shallow nonmetal pan.

2 For sauce, in a small bowl stir together butter, hot pepper sauce, and paprika. Pour sauce over chicken pieces, stirring to coat. Cover and let stand at room temperature for 30 minutes.

3 Preheat broiler. Drain chicken, reserving sauce. Place chicken pieces on the unheated rack of a broiler pan. Brush with some of the reserved sauce. Broil chicken 4 to 5 inches from the heat about 10 minutes or until light brown. Turn chicken pieces; brush again with the reserved sauce. Broil for 10 to 15 minutes more or until chicken is tender and no longer pink. Serve with blue cheese dressing.

Nutrition Facts per serving: 262 cal., 24 g total fat (6 g sat. fat), 42 mg chol., 395 mg sodium, 2 g carbo., 0 g fiber, 9 g pro. Daily Values: 7% vit. A, 2% vit. C, 3% calcium, 3% iron

Chile Chicken-Nectarine Appeteasers

Look for Oriental chile-garlic sauce in the Asian foods section of your supermarket, Asian markets, or specialty food shops.

Start to Finish: 15 minutes Makes: 16 appetizers
- 4   medium nectarines or peaches
- ½   cup shredded cooked chicken
- 2   teaspoons Oriental chile-garlic sauce or bottled chili sauce
- 2   teaspoons snipped fresh cilantro

1 Cut nectarines into quarters; remove pits. Carefully scoop out some of the fruit, leaving a ¼-inch border inside the peel. Set nectarine quarters aside. Chop the scooped-out fruit.

2 In a small bowl combine the chopped nectarine, chicken, chile-garlic sauce, and cilantro. Spoon about 1 rounded teaspoon of the chicken mixture onto each nectarine wedge.

Nutrition Facts per appetizer: 26 cal., 1 g total fat (0 g sat. fat), 4 mg chol., 12 mg sodium, 4 g carbo., 0 g fiber, 2 g pro.
Daily Values: 2% vit. A, 3% vit. C

0
net carbs

Cheese-Stuffed Pecans

To pipe the Gouda filling onto these pecan nibbles, spoon the mixture into a self-sealing plastic bag and snip off a corner.

Prep: 20 minutes Stand: 30 minutes Chill: 30 minutes Makes: 10 servings
- 1 cup finely shredded Gouda cheese (4 ounces)
- 3 tablespoons dairy sour cream
- 40 large pecan halves

1 In a medium mixing bowl let shredded cheese stand at room temperature for 30 minutes. Add sour cream. Beat with an electric mixer on medium speed until creamy.

2 Mound a scant teaspoon of the cheese mixture onto the flat side of half of the pecans. Top with remaining pecans, flat side down. Cover and chill for 30 minutes.

Nutrition Facts per serving: 102 cal., 10 g total fat (3 g sat. fat), 14 mg chol., 94 mg sodium, 1 g carbo., 1 g fiber, 4 g pro.
Daily Values: 2% vit. A, 9% calcium, 1% iron

4
net carbs

Ginger Cashews

Garam masala, a traditional Indian seasoning, flavors these fragrant nuts. It's a mix of cumin, cardamom, cinnamon, and other spices and is available in the spice section of many grocery stores and specialty foods shops.

Prep: 10 minutes Bake: 20 minutes Oven: 300°F Makes: 2 cups
- 2 cups lightly salted cashews
- 1 tablespoon butter, melted
- 1 tablespoon minced or grated fresh ginger
- 2 teaspoons garam masala

1 Line a shallow baking pan with foil or parchment paper. In a medium bowl toss together cashews, butter, ginger, and garam masala. Spread nuts in prepared pan.

2 Bake nuts in a 300° oven about 20 minutes or until golden brown and very fragrant, stirring occasionally. Serve warm or at room temperature. Store nuts in an airtight container at room temperature for up to 24 hours or in the refrigerator for 2 days. If desired, rewarm nuts on a baking sheet in a 300° oven for 5 minutes.

Nutrition Facts per 2 tablespoons: 114 cal., 10 g total fat (2 g sat. fat), 2 mg chol., 42 mg sodium, 5 g carbo., 1 g fiber, 4 g pro.
Daily Values: 1% vit. A, 7% iron

2
net carbs

Savory Macadamia Nuts

Prep: 10 minutes **Bake:** 15 minutes **Cool:** 30 minutes **Oven:** 350°F **Makes:** 2 cups

　　Nonstick cooking spray
　2　tablespoons white wine Worcestershire sauce
　1　tablespoon olive oil
　¾　teaspoon dried Italian seasoning, crushed
　¼　teaspoon salt
　⅛　teaspoon cayenne pepper
　2　cups macadamia nuts

1 Line a 13×9×2-inch baking pan with foil; lightly coat the foil with cooking spray. Set pan aside. In a small bowl stir together Worcestershire sauce, oil, Italian seasoning, salt, and cayenne pepper; set aside.

2 Spread nuts in prepared pan. Drizzle with seasoning mixture; toss gently to coat.

3 Bake in a 350° oven about 15 minutes or until nuts are toasted, stirring occasionally. Lift foil with nuts from pan. Let cool for 30 minutes. Store nuts in an airtight container at room temperature for up to 2 weeks or freeze for up to 2 months.

Nutrition Facts per ¼ cup: 258 cal., 27 g total fat (4 g sat. fat), 0 mg chol., 106 mg sodium, 5 g carbo., 3 g fiber, 3 g pro.
Daily Values: 1% vit. C, 3% calcium, 8% iron

Toasted Nuts with Rosemary

In addition to making a great snack, these herbed nuts lend a pleasant crunch to tossed salads.

Prep: 10 minutes Bake: 15 minutes Cool: 30 minutes Oven: 350°F Makes: 3 cups

Nonstick cooking spray
- 1 egg white
- 2 teaspoons snipped fresh rosemary or 1 teaspoon dried rosemary, crushed
- ½ teaspoon coarsely ground black pepper
- ½ teaspoon salt
- 3 cups walnut pieces

1 Line a 13×9×2-inch baking pan with foil; lightly coat foil with cooking spray. Set pan aside. In a medium bowl lightly beat the egg white with a fork until frothy. Add the rosemary, pepper, and salt; beat with fork until combined. Add nuts; toss to coat. Spread nuts in prepared pan.

2 Bake in a 350° oven for 15 to 20 minutes or until golden brown, stirring once. Lift foil with nuts from pan. Let cool for 30 minutes. Break up any large pieces. Store nuts in an airtight container in freezer for up to 1 month.

Nutrition Facts per tablespoon: 50 cal., 5 g total fat (1 g sat. fat), 0 mg chol., 25 mg sodium, 1 g carbo., 1 g fiber, 1 g pro.
Daily Values: 1% calcium, 2% iron

Herbed Soy Snacks

Perk up crunchy dry-roasted soybeans with one of three seasoning combos—thyme, curry, or mustard. Look for dry-roasted soybeans in your supermarket or health foods store.

Prep: 5 minutes Bake: 5 minutes Oven: 350°F Makes: 2 cups

      2 cups dry-roasted soybeans (8 ounces)
  1½ teaspoons dried thyme, crushed
   ¼ teaspoon garlic salt
   ⅛ to ¼ teaspoon cayenne pepper

1 Spread soybeans in a 15×10×1-inch baking pan. In a small bowl combine thyme, garlic salt, and cayenne pepper; sprinkle over soybeans. Bake in a 350° oven about 5 minutes or just until heated through, shaking pan once. Cool completely.

2 Store soybeans in an airtight container at room temperature for up to 1 week.

Nutrition Facts per 2 tablespoons: 75 cal., 3 g total fat (1 g sat. fat), 0 mg chol., 27 mg sodium, 4 g carbo., 2 g fiber, 7 g pro. Daily Values: 1% vit. A, 3% calcium, 5% iron

Curried Soy Snacks: Prepare as above, except omit thyme, garlic salt, and cayenne pepper. Combine 1 teaspoon curry powder and ¼ teaspoon salt; sprinkle over soybeans. Bake and store as directed.

Mustard Soy Snacks: Prepare as above, except omit thyme, garlic salt, and cayenne pepper. Combine 1½ teaspoons paprika, ½ teaspoon dry mustard, and ¼ teaspoon salt; sprinkle over soybeans. Bake and store as directed.

Cheesy Chili Popcorn

Start to Finish: 10 minutes Makes: 8 cups

- 8 cups popped popcorn
- 2 tablespoons butter, melted
- 1 teaspoon chili powder
- ⅛ teaspoon garlic powder
- 2 tablespoons grated Parmesan cheese

1 Place popcorn in a large bowl. In a small bowl stir together butter, chili powder, and garlic powder. Drizzle over popcorn; toss to coat. Sprinkle with Parmesan cheese; toss to coat. Store in a tightly covered container at room temperature for up to 3 days.

Nutrition Facts per ¹⁄₂ cup: 32 cal., 2 g total fat (1 g sat. fat), 5 mg chol., 29 mg sodium, 3 g carbo., 1 g fiber, 1 g pro.
Daily Values: 2% vit. A, 1% calcium, 1% iron

0
net carbs

Veggie Dip

Be sure to choose veggies low in carbs to go with this creamy dip. Try broccoli or cauliflower florets, sweet pepper strips, and slices of zucchini or yellow summer squash.

Start to Finish: 5 minutes Makes: about 2 cups
- 1 8-ounce tub cream cheese
- 1 8-ounce carton plain yogurt
- 1 0.4-ounce envelope ranch dry salad dressing mix (does not contain buttermilk solids)
   Vegetable dippers (such as celery sticks, broccoli or cauliflower florets, red or green sweet pepper strips, and/or cucumber slices)

1 In a medium mixing bowl beat together cream cheese, yogurt, and salad dressing mix with an electric mixer on medium speed until smooth. Serve with vegetable dippers.

Nutrition Facts per tablespoon: 28 cal., 2 g total fat (2 g sat. fat), 8 mg chol., 99 mg sodium, 0 g carbo., 0 g fiber, 0 g pro.
Daily Values: 2% vit. A, 2% calcium

Creamy Onion Dip

This version of everyone's favorite dip fits right in with low-carb eating. The assertive blue cheese kicks up the flavor.

Prep: 10 minutes Chill: 4 to 48 hours Makes: 1¾ cups
- 1½ cups dairy sour cream
- 2 tablespoons dry onion soup mix
- ½ cup crumbled blue cheese
- Snipped fresh parsley (optional)
- Assorted vegetable dippers (such as cucumber slices, zucchini slices, cauliflower florets, and/or jicama or red sweet pepper strips)

1 In a medium bowl stir together sour cream and onion soup mix. Stir in blue cheese. Cover and chill for 4 to 48 hours.

2 To serve, transfer dip to serving bowl. If desired, sprinkle with parsley. Serve with vegetable dippers.

Nutrition Facts per tablespoon: 34 cal., 3 g total fat (2 g sat. fat), 6 mg chol., 79 mg sodium, 2 g carbo., 0 g fiber, 1 g pro.
Daily Values: 36% vit. A, 2% vit. C, 3% calcium

Hot Devilish Artichoke Dip

Combine the luscious flavors of deviled eggs and artichokes, and you get this delightfully addictive dip.

Prep: 10 minutes Bake: 30 minutes Oven: 350°F Makes: about 4 cups

- 3 hard-cooked eggs, coarsely chopped
- 2 14-ounce cans artichoke hearts, drained and coarsely chopped
- 1 cup grated Parmesan cheese
- 1 cup mayonnaise
- 1 tablespoon Dijon-style mustard
   Sweet pepper strips

1 In a large bowl combine eggs, artichoke hearts, Parmesan cheese, mayonnaise, and mustard; mix well. Transfer to a 1½-quart casserole. Bake, uncovered, in a 350° oven about 30 minutes or until heated through. Serve with sweet pepper strips.

Nutrition Facts per tablespoon: 38 cal., 3 g total fat (1 g sat. fat), 13 mg chol., 86 mg sodium, 1 g carbo., 0 g fiber, 1 g pro.
Daily Values: 1% vit. A, 2% calcium, 2% iron

Salmon-Artichoke Dip

Prep: 10 minutes **Bake:** 25 minutes **Oven:** 350°F **Makes:** about 4 cups

- 2 14-ounce cans artichoke hearts, drained and chopped
- 1 cup mayonnaise
- 1 cup grated Parmesan cheese
- 1 7½-ounce can red salmon, drained, flaked, and skin and bones removed
- 2 ounces cream cheese, softened
   Vegetable dippers (such as celery sticks, broccoli or cauliflower florets, red or green sweet pepper strips, and/or cucumber slices)

1 Combine artichoke hearts, mayonnaise, and Parmesan cheese. Stir in salmon and cream cheese. Transfer to a 1-quart casserole. Bake, uncovered, in a 350° oven about 25 minutes or until heated through. Serve with vegetable dippers.

Nutrition Facts per tablespoon: 43 cal., 4 g total fat (1 g sat. fat), 6 mg chol., 99 mg sodium, 1 g carbo., 0 g fiber, 2 g pro. Daily Values: 1% vit. A, 3% calcium, 2% iron

0
net carbs

Almond-Brie Spread

If you make this spread the night before, let stand at room temperature for 30 to 45 minutes before serving.

Prep: 15 minutes Stand: 1 hour Makes: 20 servings
- 2 4½-ounce rounds chilled Brie cheese
- 2 tablespoons milk
- 3 tablespoons sliced toasted almonds
- Thin apple and/or pear slices

1 Cut the thin white covering from the Brie cheese with a vegetable peeler or small paring knife. Place cheese in a mixing bowl. Let stand at room temperature about 1 hour or until softened. Beat with an electric mixer on medium speed for 1 minute. Add milk; beat until light and smooth. Chop 2 tablespoons of the toasted almonds; stir into cheese mixture.

2 Serve immediately or cover and chill overnight or until serving time. Just before serving, sprinkle with the remaining 1 tablespoon toasted almonds. Serve with apple slices.

Nutrition Facts per serving: 51 cal., 4 g total fat (2 g sat. fat), 13 mg chol., 81 mg sodium, 0 g carbo., 0 g fiber, 3 g pro.
Daily Values: 2% vit. A, 3% calcium, 1% iron

Pesto Cheese Spread

Dress fresh veggies to the nines with this simple, sophisticated spread that's enhanced with ready-made pesto and tangy goat cheese.

Prep: 10 minutes Makes: about 1½ cups
- 1 8-ounce package cream cheese, cut up
- 4 ounces soft goat cheese (chèvre)
- ¼ cup purchased basil pesto
- 2 cloves garlic, minced
  - Assorted fresh vegetables (such as red or green sweet pepper strips; broccoli or cauliflower florets; and/or cucumber, zucchini, or yellow summer squash slices)

1 In a food processor or blender place cream cheese, goat cheese, pesto, and garlic. Cover and process or blend until smooth. If desired, transfer spread to a decorator bag with a star tip. Pipe or spoon spread onto assorted vegetables.

Nutrition Facts per tablespoon: 59 cal., 6 g total fat (3 g sat. fat), 13 mg chol., 60 mg sodium, 1 g carbo., 0 g fiber, 2 g pro.
Daily Values: 3% vit. A

Marinated Antipasto

Marinated artichoke salad provides the veggies as well as the dressing for this antipasto. The bottled salad contains artichoke hearts, pimiento, and green olives.

Prep: 20 minutes Stand: 30 minutes Chill: 1 to 2 days Makes: 10 servings

    2 12-ounce jars marinated artichoke salad, undrained
    8 ounces fontina or mozzarella cheese, cut into ½-inch cubes
    6 ounces salami, cut into ½-inch cubes
    1 teaspoon dried Italian seasoning, crushed
    ⅛ teaspoon crushed red pepper

1 In a large bowl combine the undrained artichoke salad, cheese, salami, Italian seasoning, and red pepper; toss to coat. Cover and chill for 1 to 2 days. To serve, let stand at room temperature for 30 minutes.

Nutrition Facts per serving: 195 cal., 15 g total fat (6 g sat. fat), 40 mg chol., 642 mg sodium, 4 g carbo., 1 g fiber, 11 g pro.
Daily Values: 5% vit. A, 19% calcium, 5% iron

Marinated Mozzarella with Basil

If fresh mozzarella is not available, substitute another fresh soft cheese such as queso fresco or feta. For added flavor, use olive oil infused with herbs or roasted garlic instead of plain olive oil.

Prep: 15 minutes Chill: 1 hour Makes: 14 to 16 servings

- ¼ cup fresh basil leaves
- ¼ cup olive oil
- 1 tablespoon coarsely ground black pepper
- 1 to 2 teaspoons balsamic vinegar
- 16 ounces fresh mozzarella cheese, cut into 1-inch cubes

1 Using a sharp knife, chop basil leaves. In a medium bowl combine chopped basil, oil, pepper, and vinegar. Add cheese cubes; toss gently to coat. Cover and chill for 1 hour or up to 5 days.

Nutrition Facts per serving: 126 cal., 11 g total fat (5 g sat. fat), 25 mg chol., 120 mg sodium, 1 g carbo., 0 g fiber, 6 g pro. Daily Values: 6% vit. A, 17% calcium, 1% iron

Cheese and Herb Mini Sweet Peppers

Place the tiny peppers close together on the baking sheet to help them remain upright while baking. If you prefer, line a shallow baking pan with dried beans and nestle the peppers in the beans to keep them upright.

Prep: 25 minutes Bake: 8 minutes Oven: 350°F Makes: 30 appetizers

- 30 red, yellow, and/or orange mini sweet peppers (about 12 ounces total)
- 18 ounces semisoft goat cheese (chèvre)
- ¼ cup snipped fresh chives, tarragon, basil, or thyme
  Fresh basil leaves (optional)

1 Leaving the stems intact, cut a slit along the top of each sweet pepper. Remove seeds; discard. Set sweet peppers aside.

2 In a small bowl combine goat cheese and snipped chives. Spoon cheese mixture into prepared sweet peppers. Arrange filled sweet peppers close together on a baking sheet.

3 Bake in a 350° oven for 8 to 10 minutes or until cheese is heated through and sweet peppers are crisp-tender. If desired, garnish with fresh basil.

Nutrition Facts per appetizer: 65 cal., 5 g total fat (4 g sat. fat), 13 mg chol., 88 mg sodium, 1 g carbo., 0 g fiber, 4 g pro.
Daily Values: 17% vit. A, 31% vit. C, 5% calcium, 2% iron

Cucumber-Cheese Bites

Use your imagination to make these little nibbles as simple or elaborate as you like. Fresh herbs, sliced olives, capers, and snipped roasted red sweet peppers also make colorful, low-carb toppers.

Prep: 20 minutes Makes: 20 appetizers

  2 medium cucumbers
  ½ cup semisoft cheese with garlic and herb
      Assorted toppers (such as snipped fresh chives, crumbled bacon, finely chopped hard-cooked eggs, quartered cherry tomatoes, and/or sliced green onions)

1 If desired, using a vegetable peeler or zester, remove a few lengthwise strips of peel from the cucumbers. Cut cucumbers into ½-inch slices. Spread a small amount of the cheese onto each cucumber slice. Sprinkle with assorted toppers. Serve immediately or cover and chill up to 4 hours.

Nutrition Facts per appetizer: 21 cal., 2 g total fat (1 g sat. fat), 0 mg chol., 26 mg sodium, 1 g carbo., 0 g fiber, 0 g pro. **Daily Values:** 2% vit. A, 3% vit. C

2
net carbs

Endive-Mango Appetizers

To make this stunning appetizer ahead of time, fill the endive leaves with the cream cheese mixture and arrange them on a platter. Cover and chill up to 2 hours before serving. Top with the slices of mango just before serving.

Prep: 20 minutes   Makes: about 24 appetizers

- 1   3-ounce package cream cheese, softened
- ¼   cup coarsely chopped macadamia nuts
- 2   to 3 medium Belgian endives, separated into individual leaves
- 1   large mango and/or papaya, seeded, peeled, and cut into thin strips (about 2×¾ inches)

1 In a small bowl combine cream cheese and macadamia nuts. Spread about 1 teaspoon of the cream cheese mixture into each endive leaf. Top with mango strips.

Nutrition Facts per appetizer: 29 cal., 2 g total fat (1 g sat. fat), 4 mg chol., 11 mg sodium, 2 g carbo., 0 g fiber, 0 g pro.
Daily Values: 5% vit. A, 5% vit. C

Feta-Stuffed Mushrooms

Instead of using olive oil, brush the mushrooms with the oil from the jar of dried tomatoes.

Prep: 20 minutes Bake: 10 minutes Oven: 425°F Makes: 16 appetizers

- 4 fresh portobello mushrooms (5 to 6 ounces each)
- 1 tablespoon olive oil
- 1 4-ounce package crumbled feta cheese with garlic and herb
- ¼ cup chopped pitted ripe olives
- 2 tablespoons snipped oil-packed dried tomatoes, drained

1 Clean and remove stems from mushrooms. Place mushroom caps stemmed sides up on a baking sheet. Brush with oil; set aside.

2 For filling, in a small bowl stir together the feta cheese, olives, and tomatoes. Divide filling among the mushroom caps.

3 Bake in a 425° oven about 10 minutes or until heated through. To serve, cut each mushroom cap into 4 wedges.

Nutrition Facts per appetizer: 40 cal., 3 g total fat (1 g sat. fat), 6 mg chol., 102 mg sodium, 2 g carbo., 1 g fiber, 2 g pro.
Daily Values: 1% vit. A, 1% vit. C, 5% calcium, 1% iron

4
net carbs

Portobello Pizzas

Portobello mushrooms might look exotic, but they are a variety of brown mushrooms that have been grown until the caps are 3 inches or more in diameter. They make delicious low-carb crusts for these snack-size pizzas.

Prep: 15 minutes Bake: 8 minutes Oven: 400°F Makes: 4 servings

- 4 fresh portobello mushrooms (5 to 6 ounces each)
- 5 teaspoons olive oil
   Salt and black pepper
- 1 4½-ounce round Brie cheese, thinly sliced
- ¼ cup small arugula leaves
- 4 thin tomato slices

1 Clean and remove stems from mushrooms. Brush both sides of caps with 2 teaspoons of the olive oil. Sprinkle with salt and pepper. Place mushroom caps stemmed sides up on a foil-lined baking sheet. Bake in a 400° oven for 8 to 10 minutes or until tender, turning once.

2 Remove from oven; turn caps stemmed sides up. Top each with cheese slices and arugula leaves. Drizzle some of the remaining 3 teaspoons olive oil over each. Top each with a tomato slice.

Nutrition Facts per serving: 181 cal., 16 g total fat (6 g sat. fat), 28 mg chol., 257 mg sodium, 5 g carbo., 1 g fiber, 10 g pro.
Daily Values: 8% vit. A, 10% vit. C, 6% calcium, 5% iron

Zucchini Bites

Start to Finish: 20 minutes Makes: about 36 appetizers

- 1 medium to large zucchini, cut into ¼-inch slices
- ½ of an 8-ounce tub (⅓ cup) cream cheese with salmon or ⅓ cup semisoft cheese with garlic and herb
- 1 tablespoon sliced or chopped pitted ripe olives
- 1 tablespoon snipped fresh chives

1 Pat zucchini slices dry with paper towels. Spread cream cheese over zucchini slices. Sprinkle each with olives and chives.

Nutrition Facts per appetizer: 12 cal., 1 g total fat (1 g sat. fat), 3 mg chol., 27 mg sodium, 1 g carbo., 0 g fiber, 0 g pro.
Daily Values: 1% vit. A, 2% vit. C, 1% calcium

3
net carbs

Roasted Romas with Chèvre and Pesto

A combination of pesto and chèvre makes this hors d'oeuvre fresh-tasting and creamy. Lovely as appetizers, these tomatoes also look great on dinner plates as a delicious side.

Prep: 12 minutes Bake: 7 minutes Oven: 400°F Makes: 20 appetizers

- 10 roma tomatoes, halved lengthwise (about 2 pounds)
  Salt and black pepper
- ¼ teaspoon dried thyme, crushed
- ⅔ cup purchased basil pesto
- ⅔ cup soft goat cheese (chèvre)
- 2 tablespoons snipped fresh parsley or basil

1 Sprinkle the cut sides of tomato halves with salt, pepper, and thyme. Place tomatoes, cut sides up, in a greased shallow baking pan. Bake in a 400° oven about 5 minutes or until almost tender.

2 Spoon about 1 teaspoon of the pesto onto each tomato half. Top each with about 1 teaspoon goat cheese. Bake about 2 minutes more or until cheese is softened. Sprinkle with parsley.

Nutrition Facts per appetizer: 79 cal., 6 g total fat (1 g sat. fat), 3 mg chol., 96 mg sodium, 3 g carbo., 0 g fiber, 2 g pro.
Daily Values: 6% vit. A, 14% vit. C, 1% calcium, 2% iron

Eggplant-Garlic Spread

To indulge in this tasty snack, scoop the roasted eggplant onto sweet pepper wedges. Remember to keep track of the number of these tasty appetizers you eat. It's easy to eat too many and the carbs can add up quickly.

Prep: 10 minutes Bake: 45 minutes Cool: 1½ hours Oven: 350°F Makes: 16 servings

- 1 medium eggplant (about 1 pound)
- ⅓ cup olive oil
- 2 bulbs garlic, separated into cloves, peeled, and thinly sliced
- 2 tablespoons snipped fresh flat-leaf parsley
  Sweet pepper wedges or low-carb bread, toasted and cut into quarters

1 Halve the eggplant lengthwise; brush all over with olive oil. Grease a shallow baking pan with the remaining olive oil. Place sliced garlic on the cut side of the eggplant halves. Carefully invert eggplant halves onto the prepared pan, tucking garlic slices under the eggplant.

2 Bake in a 350° oven for 45 to 60 minutes or until the skin begins to look shriveled. Turn off oven; cool eggplant in oven for 1½ hours.

3 Use a large spatula to carefully transfer eggplant halves and garlic to a serving platter, cut sides up. Sprinkle with parsley. Serve with sweet pepper wedges.

Nutrition Facts per serving: 53 cal., 5 g total fat (1 g sat. fat), 0 mg chol., 2 mg sodium, 3 g carbo., 1 g fiber, 1 g pro.
Daily Values: 1% vit. A, 3% vit. C, 1% calcium, 1% iron

Lemony Greek Olives

Keep a supply of these marinated olives in your refrigerator for a satisfying snack.

Prep: 10 minutes Chill: 1 to 2 days Makes: 10 servings
- 1 medium lemon
- 2 cups Greek black olives
- 3 tablespoons olive oil
- 1 tablespoon snipped fresh oregano or rosemary
- 2 cloves garlic, thinly sliced

1 Finely shred 1 teaspoon peel from lemon. Cut lemon in half; squeeze juice from lemon (you should have 3 tablespoons). In a medium bowl combine the lemon peel, lemon juice, olives, olive oil, oregano, and garlic; toss to coat. Cover and chill for 1 to 2 days. To serve, drain olives, discarding marinade.

Nutrition Facts per serving: 69 cal., 7 g total fat (1 g sat. fat), 0 mg chol., 235 mg sodium, 2 g carbo., 1 g fiber, 0 g pro.
Daily Values: 2% vit. A, 6% vit. C, 3% calcium, 5% iron

Spicy Marinated Olives: In a medium bowl combine 2 cups Greek black olives or green olives, ⅓ cup bottled oil and vinegar salad dressing, 1 tablespoon snipped fresh oregano or thyme, ⅛ to ¼ teaspoon crushed red pepper, and 2 cloves garlic, thinly sliced; toss to coat. Cover and chill for 1 to 2 days. To serve, drain olives, discarding marinade. Makes 10 servings.

15 Grams or Less Recipes

9
net carbs

Vegetable-Beef Soup

Prep: 5 minutes   Cook: 1½ hours   Makes: 6 servings

- 1   pound beef stew meat or boneless beef chuck roast, cut into ¾-inch cubes
- 1   tablespoon cooking oil
- 3   14-ounce cans beef broth
- 1   14½-ounce can diced tomatoes with basil, oregano, and garlic, undrained
- 1   16-ounce package frozen loose-pack broccoli, green beans, pearl onions, and red sweet pepper

1 In a Dutch oven brown meat, half at a time, in hot oil (add additional oil, if necessary). Return all meat to Dutch oven. Stir in beef broth and undrained tomatoes. Bring to boiling; reduce heat. Simmer, covered, for 1½ to 1¾ hours or until meat is tender.

2 Stir in vegetables. Return to boiling; reduce heat. Simmer, covered, about 5 minutes more or until vegetables are just tender.

Nutrition Facts per serving: 179 cal., 6 g total fat (2 g sat. fat), 45 mg chol., 1,095 mg sodium, 11 g carbo., 2 g fiber, 20 g pro.
Daily Values: 13% vit. A, 30% vit. C, 5% calcium, 17% iron

Easy Beef Chili

Start to Finish: 30 minutes Makes: 4 servings

- 1 pound lean ground beef
- 1 cup chopped onion
- 1 14½-ounce can diced tomatoes, undrained
- 1 8-ounce can tomato sauce
- ¼ cup water
- 1 tablespoon chili powder
-    Salt and black pepper

1 In a large saucepan cook ground beef and onion until meat is brown and onion is tender; drain off fat. Stir in undrained tomatoes, tomato sauce, water, and chili powder. Bring to boiling; reduce heat. Simmer, covered, for 15 minutes, stirring occasionally. Season to taste with salt and pepper.

Nutrition Facts per serving: 243 cal., 11 g total fat (4 g sat. fat), 71 mg chol., 525 mg sodium, 12 g carbo., 2 g fiber, 22 g pro.
Daily Values: 13% vit. A, 27% vit. C, 6% calcium, 17% iron

14
net carbs

Speedy Swedish Meatballs

Serve these saucy meatballs with whole green beans or spaghetti squash instead of the traditional noodles.

Start to Finish: 10 minutes Makes: 4 servings

- 1 cup water
- 1 1.1-ounce envelope mushroom gravy mix
- ¼ teaspoon black pepper
- 1 8-ounce carton dairy sour cream
- ¼ teaspoon ground allspice
- 1 16-ounce package frozen cooked meatballs, thawed
- 1 4½-ounce can sliced mushrooms, drained

1 In a large skillet combine water, gravy mix, and pepper. Cook and stir over medium-high heat for 3 to 5 minutes or until thickened and bubbly. Remove skillet from heat; stir in sour cream and allspice. Stir in meatballs and mushrooms. Return skillet to heat; heat through.

Nutrition Facts per serving: 509 cal., 42 g total fat (19 g sat. fat), 65 mg chol., 1,407 mg sodium, 17 g carbo., 3 g fiber, 17 g pro. Daily Values: 9% vit. A, 1% vit. C, 12% calcium, 6% iron

Prep: 10 minutes Grill: 8 minutes Makes: 4 servings
- 3 tablespoons low-sugar apricot preserves
- 2 tablespoons coarse-grain mustard
- 1 teaspoon cider vinegar
- ⅛ teaspoon cayenne pepper
- 1 pound cooked boneless ham, cut into four ½-inch slices

1 For glaze, in a small bowl stir together preserves, mustard, vinegar, and cayenne pepper; set aside.

2 For a charcoal grill, grill ham on the rack of an uncovered grill directly over medium-hot coals for 8 to 10 minutes or until brown, turning once and brushing occasionally with glaze. (For a gas grill, preheat grill. Reduce heat to medium-hot. Place ham on grill rack over heat. Cover and grill as above.)

Nutrition Facts per serving: 234 cal., 13 g total fat (4 g sat. fat), 65 mg chol., 1,610 mg sodium, 9 g carbo., 0 g fiber, 20 g pro. Daily Values: 1% vit. A, 6% vit. C, 2% calcium, 7% iron

15
net carbs

Smoked Pork Chop Skillet

Start to Finish: 25 minutes Makes: 4 servings
- 4 cooked smoked pork chops, cut ¾ inch thick (1¾ pounds)
- 1 16-ounce package frozen French-style green beans
- ¼ cup water
- 1½ teaspoons snipped fresh sage or ½ teaspoon dried leaf sage, crushed
- ½ cup balsamic vinegar

1 In a large nonstick skillet cook pork chops over medium heat for 3 to 5 minutes on each side or until light brown. Remove from skillet; keep warm. Add beans, water, and sage to skillet; return chops to skillet. Cover and cook over medium heat for 5 minutes.

2 Meanwhile, in a small saucepan boil balsamic vinegar gently about 5 minutes or until reduced to ¼ cup. Brush chops with vinegar; drizzle remaining vinegar over the bean mixture.

Nutrition Facts per serving: 257 cal., 14 g total fat (5 g sat. fat), 47 mg chol., 749 mg sodium, 18 g carbo., 3 g fiber, 17 g pro.
Daily Values: 10% vit. A, 20% vit. C, 5% calcium, 8% iron

Easy Sausage Soup

The carbohydrate count was calculated using a package of mixed vegetables that contains green beans, peas, carrots, and corn. Different mixtures yield slightly different carb counts.

Prep: 10 minutes Cook: 15 minutes Makes: 8 servings

- 1 pound bulk pork sausage
- 2 14½-ounce cans onion-flavor beef broth
- 1 16-ounce package frozen mixed vegetables
- 1 14½-ounce can diced tomatoes with basil, oregano, and garlic, undrained
- 1 cup water
- 2 tablespoons tomato paste
- ¼ teaspoon black pepper

1 In a 5- to 6-quart Dutch oven cook sausage until brown; drain off fat. Stir in beef broth, vegetables, undrained tomatoes, water, tomato paste, and pepper. Bring to boiling; reduce heat. Simmer, covered, about 15 minutes or until vegetables are tender, stirring occasionally.

Nutrition Facts per serving: 232 cal., 13 g total fat (5 g sat. fat), 38 mg chol., 1,004 mg sodium, 14 g carbo., 3 g fiber, 12 g pro. Daily Values: 67% vit. A, 20% vit. C, 6% calcium, 10% iron

9
net carbs

Mustard and Garlic Roasted Turkey Breast

Prep: 15 minutes **Roast:** 1¼ hours **Stand:** 10 minutes **Oven:** 325°F
Makes: 6 servings

1	2-pound turkey breast portion with bone
2	tablespoons butter, melted
¼	teaspoon salt
¼	teaspoon black pepper
¼	cup apricot or peach spreadable fruit
2	tablespoons coarse-grain brown mustard
1½	teaspoons bottled roasted minced garlic

1 Place turkey breast, bone side down, on a rack in a shallow roasting pan. Brush with 1 tablespoon of the melted butter; sprinkle with salt and pepper. Insert a meat thermometer into thickest part of the breast. The thermometer should not touch the bone.

2 For glaze, in a small bowl combine the remaining 1 tablespoon butter, spreadable fruit, mustard, and garlic; set glaze aside.

3 Roast turkey, uncovered, in a 325° oven for 1¼ to 1½ hours or until juices run clear and turkey is no longer pink (170°F), brushing with glaze several times during the last 15 minutes of roasting. Transfer turkey to a cutting board; let stand 10 to 15 minutes before carving.

Nutrition Facts per serving: 235 cal., 8 g total fat (3 g sat. fat), 104 mg chol., 254 mg sodium, 9 g carbo., 0 g fiber, 32 g pro.
Daily Values: 3% vit. A, 1% vit. C, 3% calcium, 9% iron

Pork and Plum Kabobs

Prep: 20 minutes Grill: 12 minutes Makes: 4 servings
- ⅓ cup bottled balsamic vinaigrette salad dressing
- ¼ teaspoon dried thyme, crushed
- 1 pound boneless pork loin or pork tenderloin, cut into 1-inch cubes
- 2 medium plums, seeded and quartered
- 1 medium onion, cut into thin wedges

1 In a small bowl stir together salad dressing and thyme; set aside. On 4 long metal skewers, alternately thread pork, plums, and onion wedges, leaving a ¼-inch space between pieces.

2 For a charcoal grill, grill kabobs on the greased rack of an uncovered grill directly over medium coals for 12 to 14 minutes or until done (160°F), turning once and brushing occasionally with salad dressing mixture the last 2 minutes of grilling. (For a gas grill, preheat grill. Reduce heat to medium. Place kabobs on greased grill rack over heat. Cover and grill as above.) Drizzle kabobs with any remaining salad dressing mixture.

Nutrition Facts per serving: 268 cal., 12 g total fat (3 g sat. fat), 71 mg chol., 299 mg sodium, 14 g carbo., 2 g fiber, 26 g pro.
Daily Values: 6% vit. A, 16% vit. C, 3% calcium, 5% iron

Grilled Chicken with Pineapple-Mint Salsa

Prep: 15 minutes Grill: 12 minutes Makes: 4 servings
- 1 8-ounce can crushed pineapple (juice pack), drained
- 3 tablespoons snipped fresh mint
- 2 tablespoons peach spreadable fruit
- 1 teaspoon finely chopped, seeded fresh jalapeño chile pepper*
- 4 skinless, boneless chicken breast halves
   Salt and black pepper

1 For salsa, in a small bowl combine pineapple, mint, spreadable fruit, and chile pepper. Set salsa aside.

2 Season chicken with salt and black pepper. For a charcoal grill, grill chicken on the rack of an uncovered grill directly over medium coals for 12 to 15 minutes or until chicken is no longer pink (170°F), turning once. (For a gas grill, preheat grill. Reduce heat to medium. Place chicken on grill rack over heat. Cover and grill as above). Serve with salsa.

*Note: Because hot chile peppers, such as jalapeños, contain volatile oils that can burn your skin and eyes, avoid direct contact with chiles as much as possible. When working with chile peppers, wear plastic or rubber gloves. If your bare hands do touch chile peppers, wash your hands well with soap and water.

Nutrition Facts per serving: 248 cal., 3 g total fat (1 g sat. fat), 98 mg chol., 128 mg sodium, 15 g carbo., 1 g fiber, 40 g pro.
Daily Values: 1% vit. A, 17% vit. C, 3% calcium, 11% iron

Tomato and Turkey Soup

To reduce the soup's sodium content, use chopped cooked chicken or turkey in place of the smoked turkey.

Start to Finish: 20 minutes Makes: 4 servings
- 3 14-ounce cans reduced-sodium chicken broth
- 1 14-ounce can diced tomatoes with onion and garlic or one 10-ounce can chopped tomatoes and green chile peppers, undrained
- 2 teaspoons fajita seasoning
- ¼ teaspoon black pepper
- 2 cups chopped smoked turkey breast
- 1 tablespoon snipped fresh cilantro

1 In a large saucepan combine chicken broth, undrained tomatoes, fajita seasoning, and pepper. Bring to boiling; reduce heat. Simmer, covered, for 10 minutes. Stir in turkey; heat through. Just before serving, stir in snipped cilantro.

Nutrition Facts per serving: 125 cal., 1 g total fat (0 g sat. fat), 30 mg chol., 2,062 mg sodium, 9 g carbo., 0 g fiber, 20 g pro. Daily Values: 1% vit. A, 13% vit. C, 2% calcium, 10% iron

9 net carbs

Cajun Fish Soup

Start to Finish: 20 minutes Makes: 4 servings

- 12 ounces fresh or frozen sea bass, cod, or orange roughy fillets
- 4 cups assorted stir-fry vegetables from salad bar or produce department or one 16-ounce package frozen loose-pack stir-fry vegetables
- 4 cups reduced-sodium chicken broth
- 2 teaspoons Cajun seasoning
- 1 14½-ounce can diced tomatoes, undrained

1 Thaw fish, if frozen. Rinse fish; cut into 1-inch pieces. Set fish aside. In a large saucepan combine vegetables, chicken broth, and Cajun seasoning. Bring to boiling; reduce heat. Simmer, covered, for 3 to 5 minutes or until vegetables are crisp-tender. Stir in fish and undrained tomatoes. Return to boiling; reduce heat. Simmer, covered, for 2 to 3 minutes or until fish flakes easily when tested with a fork.

Nutrition Facts per serving: 157 cal., 2 g total fat (0 g sat. fat), 35 mg chol., 968 mg sodium, 12 g carbo., 3 g fiber, 21 g pro.
Daily Values: 28% vit. A, 57% vit. C, 6% calcium, 6% iron

Manhattan-Style Clam Chowder

The potatoes are left out of this clam chowder to keep the carbohydrate count down. Bacon provides the traditional smoky flavor.

Start to Finish: 25 minutes Makes: 4 servings
- 2 6½-ounce cans minced clams
- 2 slices bacon, coarsely chopped
- 1 cup chopped celery
- 1 cup chopped onion
- 1 14½-ounce can diced tomatoes with basil, oregano, and garlic, undrained
- ¼ teaspoon salt
- ⅛ teaspoon black pepper

1 Drain canned clams, reserving juice. If necessary, add enough water to reserved clam juice to equal 2 cups. Set clams and juice aside.

2 In a large saucepan cook bacon until crisp. Remove bacon from pan, reserving drippings in pan. Drain bacon on paper towels. Cook celery and onion in reserved drippings just until tender. Stir in the reserved clam juice and the undrained tomatoes. Bring to boiling; reduce heat. Simmer, uncovered, for 5 minutes. Stir in clams, bacon, salt, and pepper; heat through.

Nutrition Facts per serving: 133 cal., 5 g total fat (3 g sat. fat), 10 mg chol., 1,026 mg sodium, 14 g carbo., 2 g fiber, 4 g pro.
Daily Values: 14% vit. A, 21% vit. C, 10% calcium, 11% iron

Grilled Shrimp Kabobs

For fiery palates, slather the kabobs with knock-your-socks-off barbecue sauce.

Prep: 20 minutes Grill: 6 minutes Makes: 4 servings
- 1 pound fresh or frozen large shrimp in shells
- 1 medium green or red sweet pepper, cut into 16 pieces
- ¼ of a medium fresh pineapple, cut into chunks
- 4 green onions, cut into 1-inch pieces
- ¼ cup bottled low-carb barbecue sauce

1 Thaw shrimp, if frozen. Peel and devein shrimp, keeping tails intact. Rinse shrimp; pat dry with paper towels. Alternately thread shrimp, sweet pepper pieces, pineapple chunks, and green onions onto 8 long metal skewers.

2 For a charcoal grill, grill kabobs on the greased grill rack of an uncovered grill directly over medium coals for 6 to 10 minutes or until shrimp are opaque, turning once and brushing with barbecue sauce halfway through grilling. (For a gas grill, preheat grill. Reduce heat to medium. Place kabobs on greased grill rack over heat. Cover and grill as above.)

Nutrition Facts per serving: 141 cal., 2 g total fat (0 g sat. fat), 140 mg chol., 268 mg sodium, 10 g carbo., 1 g fiber, 20 g pro.
Daily Values: 9% vit. A, 46% vit. C, 7% calcium, 15% iron

Parsnip-Cauliflower Mash

Prep: 10 minutes Cook: 15 minutes Makes: 4 servings
- 1 pound parsnips, peeled and sliced
- 1½ cups coarsely chopped cauliflower
- 2 cloves garlic, peeled and halved
- 2 tablespoons butter
  Salt and black pepper
- 2 to 4 tablespoons whipping cream

1 In a medium saucepan cook parsnips, cauliflower, and garlic, covered, in enough boiling salted water to cover about 15 minutes or until tender. Drain. Mash with a potato masher or beat with an electric mixer on low speed. Add butter. Season to taste with salt and pepper. Gradually beat in enough cream to make mixture slightly creamy and light.

Nutrition Facts per serving: 166 cal., 9 g total fat (6 g sat. fat), 27 mg chol., 121 mg sodium, 21 g carbo., 6 g fiber, 2 g pro.
Daily Values: 7% vit. A, 49% vit. C, 5% calcium, 4% iron

9
net carbs

Scotch Eggs

Scotch eggs are traditionally fried in deep fat, but this baked version is just as tasty and a lot simpler to make. If you like, cut the eggs in halves or quarters before serving.

Prep: 30 minutes Bake: 25 minutes Stand: 15 minutes Oven: 375°F Makes: 8 servings

- 1 pound bulk pork sausage
- 8 hard-cooked eggs (see note, page 122)
- 2 eggs
- ⅔ cup crushed shredded wheat wafers (about 13 crackers)
- ⅔ cup creamy Dijon-style mustard blend

1 Divide sausage into 8 portions. Shape each portion into a 4-inch round patty. Wrap each patty around one hard-cooked egg, covering egg completely.

3 In a small bowl beat the 2 eggs. Roll each sausage-wrapped egg in the beaten eggs; roll in crushed wafers.

4 Arrange eggs in a shallow baking pan. Bake in a 375° oven for 25 to 30 minutes or until sausage is no longer pink. Serve warm or cold with mustard blend.

Nutrition Facts per serving: 362 cal., 28 g total fat (9 g sat. fat), 298 mg chol., 688 mg sodium, 9 g carbo., 0 g fiber, 15 g pro.
Daily Values: 8% vit. A, 1% vit. C, 4% calcium, 8% iron

Raspberry Mousse

Prep: 15 minutes Chill: 3½ to 4 hours Makes: 4 servings
- ¾ cup boiling water
- 1 4-serving-size package sugar-free raspberry-flavored gelatin
- ¾ cup low-calorie cranberry juice cocktail, chilled
- 1 teaspoon finely shredded lemon peel
- 1 cup whipping cream

1 In a medium bowl combine boiling water and gelatin, stirring until gelatin is dissolved. Stir in cranberry juice cocktail and lemon peel. Cover and chill about 30 minutes or until partially set (the consistency of unbeaten egg whites).

2 In a chilled medium mixing bowl beat the whipping cream with an electric mixer on medium-high speed until stiff peaks form (tips stand straight). Fold whipped cream into gelatin mixture until combined. Spoon into 4 dessert dishes. Cover and chill for 3 to 4 hours or until firm.

Nutrition Facts per serving: 219 cal., 22 g total fat (14 g sat. fat), 82 mg chol., 39 mg sodium, 4 g carbo., 0 g fiber, 2 g pro.
Daily Values: 18% vit. A, 27% vit. C, 4% calcium

5
net carbs

Lemon-Berry Parfaits

Start to Finish: 15 minutes Makes: 4 servings
- ½ cup whipping cream
- ½ teaspoon vanilla
- 2 teaspoons finely shredded lemon peel
- 1 cup sliced fresh strawberries
- 2 tablespoons sugar-free apricot preserves, melted

1 In a chilled medium mixing bowl beat whipping cream and vanilla with an electric mixer on high speed until soft peaks form; fold in lemon peel.

2 In a small bowl toss together sliced strawberries and melted preserves. Set aside 12 of the preserve-coated berry slices. Divide the remaining berry mixture among 4 martini glasses or dessert dishes. Top each with whipped cream. Garnish with reserved berry slices. Serve immediately.

Nutrition Facts per serving: 121 cal., 11 g total fat (7 g sat. fat), 41 mg chol., 12 mg sodium, 6 g carbo., 1 g fiber, 1 g pro. Daily Values: 9% vit. A, 36% vit. C, 3% calcium, 1% iron

Wintery Ice Cream Balls

Prep: 25 minutes Freeze: 1 to 2 hours Makes: 25 (2-inch) balls
  2 cups coconut
  1 quart sugar-free vanilla ice cream

1 Place coconut in a shallow dish. Use an ice cream scoop or a large melon baller to make 2-inch ice cream balls. Roll ice cream balls in coconut, pressing firmly, until coated. Place coated ice cream balls on a cookie sheet. Freeze for 1 to 2 hours or until firm. To serve, arrange ice cream balls in serving dishes.

Nutrition Facts per ice cream ball: 74 cal., 5 g total fat (4 g sat. fat), 6 mg chol., 48 mg sodium, 8 g carbo., 1 g fiber, 2 g pro. Daily Values: 1% vit. A

7
net carbs

Spiced Baked Custard

Sugar substitute keeps this old-fashioned dessert in a low-carb meal plan. If you like, sprinkle the custards with cinnamon or nutmeg instead of the allspice.

Prep: 10 minutes Bake: 30 minutes Oven: 325°F Makes: 4 servings

    3 beaten eggs
 1½ cups milk
   ⅓ cup no-calorie heat-stable granular sugar substitute (Splenda)
 1½ teaspoons vanilla
   ½ teaspoon ground allspice

1 In a small bowl combine eggs, milk, sugar substitute, and vanilla. Beat until combined. Place four 6-ounce custard cups in a 2-quart square baking dish. Divide egg mixture among custard cups; sprinkle with allspice. Place baking dish on oven rack. Pour boiling water into baking dish around custard cups to a depth of 1 inch.

2 Bake in a 325° oven for 30 to 45 minutes or until a knife inserted near the center of each cup comes out clean. Remove cups from water. Cool slightly on a wire rack before serving. (Or cool completely in cups; cover and chill until serving time.)

Nutrition Facts per serving: 101 cal., 4 g total fat (1 g sat. fat), 161 mg chol., 97 mg sodium, 7 g carbo., 0 g fiber, 8 g pro.
Daily Values: 12% vit. A, 6% vit. C, 17% calcium, 7% iron

Minted Fresh Fruit

Prep: 25 minutes Chill: 2 hours Makes: 8 servings

- 6 cups assorted fresh fruit (such as cubed, seeded watermelon, cantaloupe, and/or honeydew melon; seedless green and/or red grapes; peeled and cubed fresh pineapple; sliced fresh strawberries; and/or peeled and sliced kiwifruit)
- 1 12-ounce can low-calorie lemon-lime carbonated beverage
- 2 tablespoons snipped fresh mint
- 1 teaspoon finely shredded orange, lime, or lemon peel

1 In a large serving bowl combine desired fruit. Stir in carbonated beverage, mint, and orange peel. Cover and chill for 2 to 6 hours, stirring occasionally.

Nutrition Facts per serving: 67 cal., 1 g total fat (0 g sat. fat), 0 mg chol., 13 mg sodium, 16 g carbo., 2 g fiber, 1 g pro.
Daily Values: 15% vit. A, 78% vit. C, 2% calcium, 3% iron

Finger Gelatin

Prep: 20 minutes   Chill: 1 hour   Makes: 40 squares
- 3   3-ounce packages sugar-free fruit-flavored gelatin
- 3   envelopes unflavored gelatin
- 4   cups water
- ½   of an 8-ounce container frozen whipped dessert topping, thawed

1 In a large bowl stir together fruit-flavored gelatin and unflavored gelatin; set aside.

2 In a medium saucepan bring water to boiling; pour into gelatin mixture in bowl. Stir constantly for several minutes or until gelatin is completely dissolved.

3 Pour mixture into a 13×9×2-inch baking pan. Chill in the refrigerator about 1 hour or until gelatin is set. Cut into squares. Arrange squares on serving platter.

4 Spoon dessert topping into a pastry bag fitted with a large star tip. Pipe a star onto each square. Cover and chill in the refrigerator to store.

Nutrition Facts per square: 34 cal., 18 mg sodium, 6 g carbo., 1 g pro.

page

Metric Information

The charts on this page provide a guide for converting measurements from the U.S. customary system, which is used throughout this book, to the metric system.

Product Differences

Most of the ingredients called for in the recipes in this book are available in most countries. However, some are known by different names. Here are some common American ingredients and their possible counterparts:

- Sugar (white) is granulated, fine granulated, or castor sugar.
- Powdered sugar is icing sugar.
- All-purpose flour is enriched, bleached or unbleached white household flour. When self-rising flour is used in place of all-purpose flour in a recipe that calls for leavening, omit the leavening agent (baking soda or baking powder) and salt.
- Light-colored corn syrup is golden syrup.
- Cornstarch is cornflour.
- Baking soda is bicarbonate of soda.
- Vanilla or vanilla extract is vanilla essence.
- Green, red, or yellow sweet peppers are capsicums or bell peppers.
- Golden raisins are sultanas.

Volume and Weight

The United States traditionally uses cup measures for liquid and solid ingredients. The chart below shows the approximate imperial and metric equivalents. If you are accustomed to weighing solid ingredients, the following approximate equivalents will be helpful.

- 1 cup butter, castor sugar, or rice = 8 ounces = ½ pound = 250 grams
- 1 cup flour = 4 ounces = ¼ pound = 125 grams
- 1 cup icing sugar = 5 ounces = 150 grams

Canadian and U.S. volume for a cup measure is 8 fluid ounces (237 ml), but the standard metric equivalent is 250 ml.

1 British imperial cup is 10 fluid ounces.

In Australia, 1 tablespoon equals 20 ml, and there are 4 teaspoons in the Australian tablespoon.

Spoon measures are used for smaller amounts of ingredients. Although the size of the tablespoon varies slightly in different countries, for practical purposes and for recipes in this book, a straight substitution is all that's necessary. Measurements made using cups or spoons always should be level unless stated otherwise.

Common Weight Range Replacements

Imperial / U.S.	Metric
½ ounce	15 g
1 ounce	25 g or 30 g
4 ounces (¼ pound)	115 g or 125 g
8 ounces (½ pound)	225 g or 250 g
16 ounces (1 pound)	450 g or 500 g
1¼ pounds	625 g
1½ pounds	750 g
2 pounds or 2¼ pounds	1,000 g or 1 Kg

Oven Temperature Equivalents

Fahrenheit Setting	Celsius Setting*	Gas Setting
300°F	150°C	Gas Mark 2 (very low)
325°F	160°C	Gas Mark 3 (low)
350°F	180°C	Gas Mark 4 (moderate)
375°F	190°C	Gas Mark 5 (moderate)
400°F	200°C	Gas Mark 6 (hot)
425°F	220°C	Gas Mark 7 (hot)
450°F	230°C	Gas Mark 8 (very hot)
475°F	240°C	Gas Mark 9 (very hot)
500°F	260°C	Gas Mark 10 (extremely hot)
Broil	Broil	Grill

*Electric and gas ovens may be calibrated using celsius. However, for an electric oven, increase celsius setting 10 to 20 degrees when cooking above 160°C. For convection or forced air ovens (gas or electric) lower the temperature setting 25°F/10°C when cooking at all heat levels.

Baking Pan Sizes

Imperial / U.S.	Metric
9×1½-inch round cake pan	22- or 23×4-cm (1.5 L)
9×1½-inch pie plate	22- or 23×4-cm (1 L)
8×8×2-inch square cake pan	20×5-cm (2 L)
9×9×2-inch square cake pan	22- or 23×4.5-cm (2.5 L)
11×7×1½-inch baking pan	28×17×4-cm (2 L)
2-quart rectangular baking pan	30×19×4.5-cm (3 L)
13×9×2-inch baking pan	34×22×4.5-cm (3.5 L)
15×10×1-inch jelly roll pan	40×25×2-cm
9×5×3-inch loaf pan	23×13×8-cm (2 L)
2-quart casserole	2 L

U.S. / Standard Metric Equivalents

⅛ teaspoon = 0.5 ml	
¼ teaspoon = 1 ml	
½ teaspoon = 2 ml	
1 teaspoon = 5 ml	
1 tablespoon = 15 ml	
2 tablespoons = 25 ml	
¼ cup = 2 fluid ounces = 50 ml	
⅓ cup = 3 fluid ounces = 75 ml	
½ cup = 4 fluid ounces = 125 ml	
⅔ cup = 5 fluid ounces = 150 ml	
¾ cup = 6 fluid ounces = 175 ml	
1 cup = 8 fluid ounces = 250 ml	
2 cups = 1 pint = 500 ml	
1 quart = 1 litre	